Aaron M. Powell

Personal Reminiscences of the Anti-Slavery and Other Reforms and Reformers

Aaron M. Powell

Personal Reminiscences of the Anti-Slavery and Other Reforms and Reformers

ISBN/EAN: 9783744714693

Printed in Europe, USA, Canada, Australia, Japan

Cover: Foto ©Suzi / pixelio.de

More available books at **www.hansebooks.com**

Personal Reminiscences

OF

THE ANTI-SLAVERY AND OTHER REFORMS AND REFORMERS.

BY

AARON M. POWELL.

PUBLISHED BY

ANNA RICE POWELL,
PLAINFIELD, N. J.

NEW YORK:
CAULON PRESS, NO. 20 VESEY STREET.

1899.

Sincerely thy friend,
Aaron M. Powell.

Dedication.

—

TO THE

YOUNG

TO WHOM THE WRITER OF THESE REMINISCENCES

HAD ALREADY DEDICATED THEM

IN HIS HEART.

INTRODUCTION.

———

" The man is the spirit he works in ; not what he did, but what he became."—*Carlyle.*

———

I have been asked to write an introduction to this volume of reminiscences by my friend Aaron M. Powell, which was left unfinished at the time of his sudden death; and at the request of many friends is now placed before the public by loving survivors of his love.

If the work could have been completed by himself no introduction by another hand would be in place, but as it is, perhaps one who has had for a few years the privilege of some personal intimacy with him, succeeding a familiarity with his career for more than forty years, may fitly write that which he could not himself have written, but which is not only accurate testimony to a rare and noble life, but part of the history of an eventful epoch and of a generation of historic workers, which with his departure may be said to be almost gone.

Fifty years ago the author of this volume was approaching manhood at a time not understood, not appreciated then, but which proved to be a crucial time in the life of the nation and even an eventful period in human history. The career of African slavery under the flag of the American republic was—though it seemed far otherwise—drawing to a close. In the ten years preceding the civil war, it seemed to the world as if the power of slavery had so grown and strengthened that it was established as the ruler of the nation, the dictator not alone of its governmental policy but also of its social life ; and it even assumed to step between man and his Maker in its control of the church. But though to the outward eye its power seemed absolute and the theory of "government of the people by the people and for the people" a hollow sham hastening to its end, yet such was not the Divine decree. In the order of Providence great spiritual forces were working—even though unseen—and the deadly calm which prevailed was but the precursor of that which may well be called the tempest of the century.

For a quarter of a century preceding the war a small band of heroic men and women had dedicated their lives and all their powers to waging war against the giant evil, at the sacrifice of all that seemed most precious in life ; for such sacrifice was required of all who were active in the heroic and apparently hopeless crusade against human slavery. The share in the great work of stirring the conscience and the brain of the nation, which was performed by the so called Garrisonian abolitionists, is not yet accurately apportioned by the deliberate judgment of mankind. But as the years roll by the perspective greatens, and that which was not clearly discerned by contempory vision, nay ! which was at the time denied by a time-serving, acquiescent

public opinion, seems great, even sublime—
not only in its consecrated service, but in the
surpassing grandeur of the results attained.
These results followed the labors and the
prophecies of the little band referred to with
startling rapidity, and as the single fife and
drum which accompanied John Brown's body
to the grave on that bleak December day of
'59 was the advance guard of a million of men
in arms, so this company of true hearted men
and women were the undoubted pioneers of a
movement which convulsed the nation, and in
which Slavery went down in fire and blood.

From the present point of view, not yet
remote enough to be accounted that of impartial history, there is a growing recognition of
the moral greatness and the spiritual elevation
and fervor amounting perhaps to Apostleship,
which characterized that little band of radical
abolitionists who, casting aside all considerations of policy and rejecting all compromises
with evil, "cried aloud and spared not."
Church, State, Society, were all against them—
public opinion not only disallowed but ridi-

culed their demands, and, judged by human standards, it seemed quixotic for this little company to array its feeble forces against the apparently impregnable stronghold of Slavery, supported as it was by the wealth, respectability and power of the nation. But again, and signally, was it shown that " One with God is a majority."

This is not the place nor the season to attempt to measure the extent and value of their work. But the fact is admitted that some of the noblest men and women of the age, both in spiritual and intellectual endowments, gave up their lives to the cause, sacrificing thereto everything that seemed valuable of life's gifts.

Garrison, a man of considerable intellectual and of high moral endowments, with a spirit stern for the right as Luther's, was the leader and organizer; and around him gathered a little band, unexcelled in human history for singleness of purpose and purity of life, each seemingly equipped for some special service in the great crusade.

Wendell Phillips, styled by Bryce, in his American Commonwealth, one of the first orators of the century, was naturally the orator of the cause, to which in his young manhood he had dedicated a life overflowing with promise ; and Whittier, the poet, and our own Lucretia Mott, were other leaders of that little company, who, to the amazement of their generation in their devotion to a special mission, worked not by the methods of man and eschewed all human policy. A large proportion of these warriors of the spirit were members of the peaceable Society of Friends. Contemporary with them, though in a sense following after—perhaps equalling them in devotion though differing in method—were Sumner, the statesman ; Greeley, the editor ; Beecher, the preacher ; Curtis, the accomplished scholar and ideal Christian gentleman —the Sir Philip Sidney of his time—and many others, who formed the vanguard of the movement which led to the formation of the Republican party. This larger company sought the same ends by what would appear to be more reasonable methods, in and through political action.

It is useless to attempt now to judge between these differing moral forces. Each no doubt had its place in the Divine economy; but without assuming to anticipate the verdict of history, it would seem already as if the uncompromising Garrisonian abolitionists, who in the estimation of the prudent, level headed judgment of their day, were impolitic, impracticable, even dangerous members of society, were in reality the apostles and prophets of the new era about to dawn upon human history, when man's wisest methods of policy were set at naught and spiritual forces prevailed in the giant convulsion of the age.

Even at this writing the newspapers chronicle the occasion of the re-burial—August 30th—of the remains of John Brown's associates by the side of their leader at North Elba, N. Y.

A distinguished company gathered, and addresses were made by noted speakers, among them one by the most distinguished

Bishop of the Episcopal church ; and thirty-five hundred voices joined in singing

"John Brown's body lies a mouldering in the grave," and

" Onward, Christian soldiers."

Truly, as Lowell wrote—

" Humanity sweeps onward."

Aaron M. Powell was among the very youngest of the radical anti-slavery workers, having come to manhood about ten years before the end. The battle for human rights was then being intensely waged, and the young man who had in his youth given up his cherished ambition for a college education in order to devote his life to the cause of the slave, was one of the most faithful and energetic of the younger anti-slavery workers, during the decade which followed and immediately preceded the bursting of the fire, which had smouldered for a generation, into the flame of civil war, in which human slavery was consumed and a new career opened, not alone for the African race but for the American republic.

While we cannot accurately indicate the respective proportions of the work done by God's servants in carrying out the Divine decrees, it may now be said that the little band of men and women referred to, who in their devotion to the high ideal of human liberty received only the scorn and obloquy of their generation, have been proven to be worthy of a high place in history among the noted reformers of all time. Most of them lived to witness the fruitage of their life's efforts and to enter the promised land of their desires.

The author of this volume was still a young man when the great work was accomplished to which he had consecrated his life. Indeed it proved that one-half of his life had yet to be lived when human slavery went down in the shock of civil war. The baptismal fire through which he had passed, and the heroic companionship of his young life had qualified him for a service of no common order, and for a third of a century afterward he lived among us, not as other men live, attentive to duty perhaps as the call comes to them, yet immersed in the affairs of life and taking not improperly their share of life's good things. From the beginning to the end, his proved to be a consecrated life. With abilities of a high order, equipped for success in almost any field he might select of human effort, he lived a life apart from usual ambitions, regulating his conduct by standards which, though the wisdom of the world might account them foolishness, seem now not far removed from saintly, in their requirements of complete consecration to the service of God, in the service of His downtrodden and erring creatures.

Worldly aims to him possessed no attractions : his sole desire seemed to be to follow in the footsteps of his Master. And so the prime of his manhood and his declining years as well were devoted solely to his Master's work. All good causes appealed to him, but most of all those that being least popular stood most in need. The cause of the colored race, of the Indian, of peace, of temperance, of education—especially higher education in the

Society of Friends—and above all the personal purity movement, which, with so many friends, had but few to openly champion it ; all these received his earnest support, and the last named his unquestioned leadership.

Right in the midst of service the call came to him to come up higher. Sudden and saddenning was the shock to his loving friends and to a wider circle, but the sorrow had an inevitable touch even of rejoicing, in the knowledge that he who had worked so long and faithfully for the Master was translated at once to His presence without a pang of suffering.

While in one sense the unfinished state of these reminiscences is to be regretted, in another they appeal even more strongly to us as the interrupted speech of our friend— interrupted only—not ceased, for we shall hear his voice again.

ISAAC H. CLOTHIER.

Harbour Entrance, Jamestown, R. I.,
September 1st, 1899.

CONTENTS.

CONTENTS.

ILLUSTRATIONS.

CHAPTER I.

———

My attention was first called to the subject
of slavery, in my boyhood, by an illustrated
pamphlet, upon the first page of which was
shown the picture of a negro slave woman,
with her baby in her arms, who was being
severely whipped by a cruel slave-driver,
or plantation overseer, until her bared back
was lacerated, and blood was flowing from the
wounds. She was in a cotton field at work
with a hoe with other slaves, negro men and
women, and had ventured at the end of the
row to lay down her hoe and take up her babe
to nurse it. This interfered with her field
work, offended the brutal overseer, and hence
her cruel punishment. Though myself but a
child at the time, this picture, with the interpretation of it which my mother gave to me,
as she read from the anti-slavery pamphlet
which had found its way into our rural home,
in the valley of the Hudson, made a deep and

lasting impression upon my memory, which the lapse of more than half a century has not sufficed to efface. It gave me a vivid conception of the cruelty and injustice involved in the odious system of "property in man," ownership of men and women, created in the image of God.

The American Anti-Slavery Society, of which William Lloyd Garrison was the pioneer and founder, was organized at a National Anti-Slavery Convention held in Philadelphia in 1833, when I was but a little more than one year old. Through the earlier efforts of John Woolman, Elihu Coleman, Anthony Benezet, Benjamin Lundy and others, chiefly members of the Religious Society of Friends, a strong feeling against slavery had been created, and slavery among Friends, as a Religious Society, had been abolished, and the ownership of slaves had been made a disciplinary offense. It was with the enunciation of the doctrine of "immediate and unconditional emancipation, the right of the slave and the duty of the master," as voiced, with great moral emphasis and in most uncompromising terms by William Lloyd Garrison and supported by his early coadjutors, that the effective modern anti-slavery movement, which culminated in the final abolition of slavery, may be said to have been inaugurated.

My acquaintance with the American Anti-Slavery Society and its work began in 1850, in connection with a visit from Stephen S. and Abby Kelley Foster, as its representatives, for a series of Anti-Slavery meetings at Ghent, Columbia County, N. Y., the home of my boyhood. They were guests of my father and mother at this time. These were the first meetings of the kind ever held there, and theirs were the first anti-slavery addresses to which I had ever listened. I was at once deeply interested in their very earnest and stirring appeals in behalf of the greatly wronged and outraged slave. I was perhaps even more profoundly impressed by their conversation upon the subject in our home, than by their public addresses, eloquent, powerful, and moving as they were. Just before their coming to us I had been reading, with absorbed interest, the Journals of George Fox, the pioneer and founder of the Religious Society of Friends. Even so long ago as his early labors in Barbadoes his preaching against slavery was so pronounced as to alarm the slaveholders and cause them to forbid the attendance of his meetings by the negroes. He also strongly opposed war, and maintained a very vigorous controversy with the corrupt priesthood of the time. Stephen S. Foster, beside being a most outspoken, uncompromising opponent of slavery, was also a non-resistant, opposed to all war, and a tremendous critic of compromising, pro-slavery priests and politicians. Fresh from the reading of Fox's Journals, it seemed, as I listened ·to Stephen's stirring addresses and conversation, as though, verily, George Fox had come again! He was deemed a great troubler in the pro-slavery Israel, and was often confronted with mob violence. Like Fox, he was sometimes dragged out of meetings and churches at the imminent peril of his life, and more than once imprisoned. He used

ABBY KELLEY FOSTER.

sometimes humorously to claim that he really had very small combativeness, but that what he had was very active! Educated for the ministry in the Congregational Church of New England, he became a "come-outer," and consecrated himself, fearlessly and most unselfishly, to the slave's redemption. Harsh and formidable as he often appeared on the public platform, he was in private a most genial, gentle and lovable companion, except to evil-doers and their apologists, political and religious, to whom he was everywhere and always a terror.

Abby Kelley Foster was, at the time of this to me very memorable visit, in the prime of life, a woman of marked intellectual ability, a gifted, eloquent speaker, with rare moral courage and the martyr spirit. She was of the New England Quaker stock, and as a young woman, before enlisting in the anti-slavery crusade was a Massachusetts teacher. It was at one of the historic anti-slavery conventions, held in 1839 in Pennsylvania Hall, Philadelphia, confronted with a furious mob, and addressed with much difficulty and peril, by Angelina Grimke, Maria Weston Chapman of Boston, Lucretia Mott and others, that Abby Kelley, a delegate from Massachusetts, spoke with such power for the slave, that she was strongly urged to enter the anti-slavery lecturing field, which she did soon after.

It was during the prosecution of their anti-slavery labors, in the midst of much persecution, that the acquaintance between herself and Stephen Foster began, which ripened into a true and beautiful marriage. Theirs was a union of close sympathy and, on the part of each, with a large measure of individuality. Thoroughly familiar with the legal and political aspects of the subject of slavery, logical and argumentative beyond the average, few men could hold their own in discussion with Abby on the anti-slavery platform. At that time a woman's voice, outside of a Friends' meeting, was very rarely heard in public. Sarah and Angelina Grimke, members of the Society of Friends, natives of

South Carolina and reared in the midst of slavery, had come North to reside in Philadelphia and to advocate emancipation. They were the real pioneers among women on the public anti-slavery platform. The voice of Lucretia Mott had also occasionally been heard pleading for the slave in meetings of the general public. Angelina Grimke, who became the wife of Theodore D. Weld, and Sarah Grimke had retired from active public anti-slavery service before my own connection with the American Anti-Slavery Society. Though I did not know them intimately, I had the pleasure of making their acquaintance in later years, as of Mr. Weld, who was an able and eloquent anti-slavery advocate. I once visited with much interest the famous school founded by Mr. Weld at Eagleswood. Perth Amboy, N. J. His lovely relations with the young people about him were a delight to behold. The club women, who, in large numbers, are now so easily at the front on public platforms, can scarcely realize in full their debt of obligation to such early pioneers as the Grimke sisters, Lucretia Mott and Abby Kelley Foster ; and later, Lucy Stone, Antoinette Brown Blackwell, Elizabeth Cady Stanton and Susan B. Anthony, for making possible for them their present comparatively smooth and pleasant public pathway.

As late even as 1850, the rather slow and conservative people of the Hudson River Valley, many of them descendants of the Holland-Dutch settlers, with little conception of equality of rights for women, were not a little shocked and scandalized by Abby Kelley Foster's able and fearless public discussion and criticism of pro-slavery men and measures. Some of them who knew me, and my parents, and of the very deep interest awakened in me in the anti-slavery cause, expressed solicitude lest I was being led astray and to ruin by a "vile and dangerous woman!" She was herself quite cognizant of the icy coldness of this region towards their anti-slavery efforts, and writing of it in a letter to the *National Anti-Slavery Standard*, dated Hudson, N.

Y., February 7, 1850, she says : " It seemed almost like going into the arctic circle to sow wheat." In Hudson their meetings were much disturbed, and unmerchantable eggs were thrown by the mob, several of which struck my uncle Aaron C. Macy, who was their friend, and whose name I bear.

One legacy of this first visit of Stephen and Abby Foster in our home was the weekly visits of the *National Anti-Slavery Standard* and *The Liberator.* They were read by me with the greatest interest, and became the basis of my anti-slavery education, commenced with the visit of the Fosters. This was during the Fugitive Slave Law era, an acute period of the anti-slavery agitation.

It was in 1851, in my nineteenth year, that I attended my first anti-slavery convention. This convention was arranged for, under the auspices of the American Anti-Slavery Society, by Stephen and Abby Foster, and was held in the Congregational Church, at Union Village, Washington County, N. Y. Beside the Fosters, it was attended and addressed also by George Thompson of England, then on his second visit to the United States, and by Sojourner Truth, the remarkable negro woman, herself formerly a slave in the State of New York. It thus happened that, before I had met William Lloyd Garrison and Wendell Phillips, I was brought into contact with the rarely gifted British anti-slavery champion. He came to this convention direct from Springfield, Mass., where he had been outrageously treated by a furious pro-slavery mob. His face was radiant with good cheer, and his voice melodious and the most eloquent I had ever listened to. It seemed to me then well nigh incomprehensible how any one could come from such mobocratic confusion and uproar, attended with great risk of personal violence, and yet bring to us so much of geniality and spiritual sunshine! I have since attended many conventions with varying conditions, sometimes turbulent, but probably never one so momentous and influential as affecting my own life. Anxious as I was, with my quickened and growing interest in

GEORGE THOMPSON.

the anti-slavery movement, to share this convention, I found the way difficult, and it seemed as though I would be obliged to forego it. My father, who had consented to receive Stephen and Abby Foster in our home, was not at that time, as he afterwards became, in sympathy with the anti-slavery cause. Though not specially active in politics, he was associated with the Democratic, or pro-slavery party, concerning which he and Stephen had prolonged and vigorous discussions, in which, as I listened, I could but feel that my father was at a great disadvantage. After the visit and meetings were over and the Fosters had gone, observing how deeply interested I had become in the subject, and moved somewhat also, doubtless, by the counsel and suggestions of some of our prejudiced pro-slavery friends and acquaintances, he sought to dissuade me from being "too much carried away by the Abolitionists." He was opposed to my going to the convention ; but, seeing how much my heart was set upon it, and with the entreaty of my mother in my behalf, finally did not forbid it. It was arranged that, going by way of Albany, I should pay a visit to some relatives and friends, members of the Society of Friends, who were also interested in the anti-slavery movement, in Saratoga, and go with them, about twenty miles distant, to the anti-slavery convention. It was during an intermission, between the sessions, seated in earnest conversation with a group of these Saratoga and Washington County friends, that Sojourner Truth, who had been standing alone by the pulpit, came slowly down the aisle to us, about midway in the church, and reaching out her long, bony arm, placed her big black hand on my head, saying as she did so, with prophetic tone, in her peculiar dialect, "I'se been a lookin' into your face, and I sees you, in the futur', pleadin' our cause!" In later years, as I visited these friends for anti-slavery meetings I was frequently reminded by them of Sojourner's prophecy.

Sojourner Truth, sometimes called the "Lybian Sibyl," was born in Ulster County,

New York, in 1787, and was a slave until slavery was legally abolished in the Empire State in 1827. Scars upon her body were in evidence as to the cruelty of the system of which she had been a victim. She was a woman of much native intelligence, of powerful voice, with great originality of expression, which, combined with her peculiar dialect, a quaint humor, and picturesque appearance, made her always a welcome speaker in the anti-slavery meetings. Her stirring originality was well illustrated on one occasion which has been often referred to, when she was in attendance at a convention in which Frederick Douglass was making a speech. He had dwelt at length with a tone of discouragement upon the many difficulties and obstacles with which the anti-slavery movement had to contend, tending to create a feeling of despondency on the part of his hearers, when Sojourner, who was in the back part of the hall, interrupted him, asking in a stentorian tone : " Frederick, is God dead?" It was like an electric shock, and instantly changed the current of thought and feeling in the convention. The last years of her life were passed mainly in Battle Creek, Michigan, and an interesting volume chronicles many of the events and incidents of her remarkable career.

George Thompson paid three visits to the United States. The first was in 1834, a year after the abolition of slavery in the British West India Islands, which Lord Brougham declared, in the House of Lords, that George Thompson had done more than any other man to achieve. The second was in 1850, when the Fugitive Slave Law excitement ran high. The third was in 1864, the year following President Lincoln's historic Emancipation Proclamation. On the occasion of his first visit so violent was the pro-slavery feeling against him as an abolitionist and an intermedling "foreigner" that he was often in imminent danger, and was finally obliged to leave the country and return to England. Like Mr. Garrison, he was of humble origin, but with a great natural oratorical gift, which was cultivated in a debating club, and became publicly known through his anti-slavery labors in Great Britain. He came to the front rank among the great orators of his time and achieved an international reputation as a large hearted, consecrated philanthropist. Despite the pro-slavery hatred with which he was confronted on his first visit to this country, multitudes listened to him with eager interest, and his enemies were often discomfited by his quick repartee. In one of his meetings in Boston, when some riotous Southerners who were present cried out: " We wish we had you at the South. We would cut your ears off, if not your head !" Mr. Thompson promptly replied : " Would you ? Then I should cry out all the louder, ' He that *hath* ears to hear let him hear !' " Rev. S. J. May, who mentions this incident in his " Recollections of the Anti-Slavery Conflict," says of this reply : " It was irresistible. I believe the Southerners themselves joined in the rapturous applause." One of his memorable addresses at the Union Village Convention, where I first listened to him, in 1851, on his second visit to the United

States, abounded specially with humorous sallies and anecdote, carrying the convention, his pro-slavery hearers and others, enthusiastically with him. It was during a recess of Parliament, of which Mr. Thompson had been elected a member, to represent the Tower Hamlets Constituency, London, that his second visit to this country was made. Ostensibly for a period of needed rest, it proved to be instead a season of great activity for him, so great was the demand for his services in that critical era of the anti-slavery movement. Except at Springfield, Mass., where, as previously noted, he was confronted with a disgraceful mob, he was everywhere welcomed with enthusiasm and delight.

There was a singular appropriateness in the time chosen for his third and last visit to this country, following the official edict of emancipation, and at the final culmination of the great "irrepressible conflict," with which he had long been so closely linked in sympathy, and so conspicuously and honorably identified. Whereas on his first American visit thirty

years earlier he had been fiercely mobbed,
hunted and driven from the country at the
peril of his life, now he was received with distinguished consideration by President Lincoln,
by many Senators and Representatives in the
halls of Congress, and by many other eminent
citizens, official and unofficial. He was, with
Mr. Garrison, made the nation's guest by
Edwin M. Stanton, the Secretary of War at
that time, to visit Charleston, and witness the
re-raising of the flag at Fort Sumter. It
was my own privilege to be present on that
historic occasion, to which I shall again refer.
I recall vividly, as I write these lines, the
joyous glow of Mr. Thompson's handsome
face, as standing by the side of Mr. Garrison,
the two anti-slavery pioneers, with Henry
Ward Beecher and others, within the walls of
the Fort, pulled the rope which restored the
original flag to the place from which, at the
beginning of the war, four years before, it had
been hauled down at the bidding of the leaders of the slaveholders' rebellion!

My last interview with George Thompson,

most pathetic, was in his own home, at Leeds, in England, in the autumn of 1877. I was returning from Geneva, Switzerland, where I had been attending the first International Congress at which was organized the International Federation for the Abolition of State Regulation of Vice. En route from London, and before sailing from Liverpool for New York, I paid a brief visit to Scotland and the North of England, including Leeds and York. At Edinburgh I was the guest of Elizabeth Pease Nichol, in her most hospitable home at Huntly Lodge. She was the very intimate, long-time friend of George Thompson, as also of William Lloyd Garrison and Wendell Phillips, and a deeply interested, sympathetic co-worker for many years with the American Anti-Slavery Society. The time at my command was limited, but it was arranged that in journeying from Edinburgh to York, I should stop over at Leeds, for an hour with George Thompson. He was then, as he had been for a considerable period, an almost helpless invalid from paralysis. His vocal organs were much affected and talking was difficult for him. Mrs. Nichol had written him in advance of my coming and when, so that he was expecting me. As I was shown into his chamber he was sitting up, but I was much shocked by the painful contrast as I then saw him, and my memory of him, in his prime, with his splendid physique a quarter of a century earlier. He also seemed confused and disappointed as he saw me. He was, as he with difficulty told me, expecting to see a colored man, when my name was announced. There was associated with the anti-slavery office in New York for many years a colored man by the name of William P. Powell, with whom, on his visits to the United States, he had become pleasantly acquainted. The mention of my name, in connection with the *National Anti-Slavery Standard* by Mrs. Nichol, in writing to him, had given him the impression that it was the colored Powell who was coming to see him. Presently his memory rallied, and he recalled incidents of the anti-slavery convention where we first met, and of our subsequent meetings in New York, Philadelphia and elsewhere. After a little time, as his mind reverted to the anti-slavery associations and experiences, a measure of the old time fire came back to his eye, somewhat of his eloquence of speech returned and he had many questions to ask, accompanied by many suggestive comments, concerning persons and events of the familiar past. The hour passed quickly, and when the time came that I must leave he was conversing eagerly, and holding my hand, managed to walk with me to the head of the stairway, there to say with much emotion his farewell. He had been visited a few weeks previous, by William Lloyd Garrison, on the occasion of his last visit to England, and they then had their last meeting. He lingered till the following year, and October 7, 1878, passed on to the larger life beyond.

CHAPTER II.

My active service in connection with the American Anti-Slavery Society, as a Lecturing Agent, commenced in the autumn of 1854. Following the visit of the Fosters and my first anti-slavery convention referred to in the previous chapter, I became a student at the State Normal School, at Albany, N. Y. My boyhood ideal was to prepare myself thoroughly for teaching, and thus to earn the money which would enable me to have a college course, at Antioch College, then under the Presidency of Horace Mann. Horace Mann was at that time a conspicuous representative of American educational interests, and as such, an inspiration to many young men. He was also of liberal anti-slavery tendencies. It was during the summer vacation of 1854 that, by invitation, I made my first visit to Worcester, Mass., the home of Stephen and Abby Foster ; and, with them, visited Boston. It happened that at the time of this visit the Fosters had an engagement to address an anti-slavery meeting at Stoneham, a suburb of Boston, and I was invited to accompany them. It also chanced after our arrival at Stoneham that Stephen was quite disabled for the time by a sudden illness and unable to take the part expected of him in the meeting. In the State Normal School at Albany I was a member of one of its Literary Societies and, as such, had taken part in its debates. The slavery question, especially the Fugitive Slave Law, then a burning public question, had claimed much of our attention. While it was for the most part debated in a perfunctory way by the young men, merely for the sake of the training in public speaking, in my own case it was quite otherwise. Choosing what was then the minority and unpopular side in the discussions, what I said was from deep and earnest conviction against the unspeakable wickedness, cruelty and injustice of slavery and slave hunting. This also soon fixed my status with the students and professors as *the* " anti-slavery fanatic" of my class. Abby knowing of this experience, and the same questions being uppermost at the Stoneham meeting, asked me, in the unexpected absence of Stephen, to address the meeting. Though I had never before undertaken such a responsibility, and had much shrinking therefrom, I was, by my deep interest in the subject, moved to comply with her request. Of what I actually said I have no distinct remembrance at this distance of time. The following day we attended in Boston a meeting of the Executive Committee of the American Anti-Slavery Society, at No. 21 Cornhill, for so many years the real anti-slavery headquarters, not alone for New England but for the nation. It was at this memorable meeting that I first met William Lloyd Garrison, Wendell Phillips, Francis Jackson, Maria Weston Chapman, Edmund Quincy, Eliza Lee Follen, Charles F. Hovey, Rev. Samuel May, Jr., and others of that remarkable group of pioneer American Abolitionists. In the course of the meeting I was introduced by Abby, with mention of my part

in the Stoneham meeting of the day before.
I was very kindly welcomed, as somebody
said, as " Abby Kelley Foster's only convert
in the Hudson River Counties!" The request was also made of me that, in view of
the importance of the crisis then pending in
the anti-slavery movement, and the great
need of more laborers, I would suspend my
studies at the State Normal School, tempor-
arily, and assist, as a Lecturing Agent, in the
work of the Abolitionists, while the crisis continued. Alas! the " crisis " did not end until
slavery itself was ended, and, as a consequence, I never finished my work at the State
Normal School, and never even began, what
I fully intended, and greatly desired, the college course at Antioch.

I did not at once promise to enter the
anti-slavery lecture field as one of the Society's
lecturing agents, but said I would consider it,
and on my return home would see if I could
make some appointments for meetings on my
own account, and then if, with a little experience, I felt that I could really be of service,

WILLIAM LLOYD GARRISON.

I would undertake for a time the lecturing mission.

WILLIAM LLOYD GARRISON.

Of the Executive Committee meeting which I have mentioned, the central figure was William Lloyd Garrison. Strong and gifted as were the other members, each in his or her own way, with a marked individuality, his was the master spirit of the remarkable group. For full details of his great career I must refer my young readers, for whom chiefly these " Reminiscences " are written, to " The Story of His Life," which is also, in large part, a history of the American anti-slavery movement, admirably presented in four large volumes, by his sons, Wendell Phillips Garrison and Francis Jackson Garrison. Born in Newburyport, Mass., in 1805, of humble parentage, his educational opportunities were very meagre, limited mainly to a brief period at the Grammar School. Becoming finally an apprentice in the printing office of the Newburyport *Herald*, this proved to be for him the right place at the right time, and here he had a practical training, most valuable as a substitute for school and college. He gained experience in writing for the *Herald*, and subsequently established and became editor of the Newburyport *Free Press*. It was while editing and publishing the *Free Press* that he discovered John G. Whittier, then an unknown farmer's boy, at work, as such, upon his father's farm, a few miles distant. It was after he had sold the *Free Press*, and was at work as a printer in Boston, that he met Benjamin Lundy, editor of the *Genius of Universal Emancipation*, a pioneer abolitionist, of the school of John Woolman, and like him a member of the Society of Friends. For a brief period Mr. Garrison became editor of *The National Philanthropist*, a total abstinence paper; and subsequently, in 1828, of the *Journal of the Times*, at Bennington, Vt., a paper friendly to the re-election of John Quincy Adams as President, and favoring anti-slavery, temperance, peace and moral reform. It was the following year, 1829, that

Benjamin Lundy made another journey, on foot, from Baltimore to Bennington for a second interview with Mr. Garrison; this time to invite him to edit the *Genius of Universal Emancipation*, while he (Lundy) would travel and solicit subscriptions for the paper. This invitation was accepted, and in September, 1829, Mr. Garrison began his editorial work in Baltimore, in a co-partnership with Lundy. He had become very deeply interested in behalf of the enslaved, his treatment of the subject was more pro-- nounced and aggressive than Lundy's, so that more rapidly than the latter could secure them, were the subscribers to the *Genius* frightened away by him. At the end of five months, (March 1830) the paper, and with it the co-partnership of Lundy and Garrison, had to be discontinued. The *Genius of Universal Emancipation* was subsequently resumed, by Lundy, as a small monthly in Washington.

In consequence of several editorial strictures in the *Genius* upon the owner and captain of a Newburyport (Mass.) vessel, for carrying a cargo of slaves and thus promoting the domestic slave trade, Mr. Garrison was arrested, tried and imprisoned for libel, in a Baltimore jail, for a period of seven weeks. Through the kindness of Arthur Tappan, of New York, who volunteered to pay his fine, he was finally released from the jail. While in prison he was busy with his pen, and improved the opportunity to prepare three anti-slavery lectures. These he sought in vain, on leaving the jail, an opportunity to deliver in Baltimore. He then started Northward, poor and penniless, and, stopping in Philadelphia, arrangements were made for him to deliver his lectures in the Franklin Institute. They were attended mainly by members of the Society of Friends and colored people. Among those who attended his lectures and gave him a kindly welcome were James and Lucretia Mott. En route to Boston he also lectured in New York, New Haven and Hartford, the major portion of his hearers being colored people. Arrived in

Boston, no church or meeting-house could be had in which he could lecture. In response to an advertisement in a Boston newspaper, Julien Hall, belonging to the Abner Kneeland " Infidel Society," was offered for the purpose, and he gave therein his series of anti-slavery lectures, October 1830. Among those who listened to them were Dr. Lyman Beecher (the father of Henry Ward Beecher and Harriet Beecher Stowe), Dr. Gannett, Rev. Samuel J. May and A. Bronson Alcott. Then followed the publication, in Boston, of *The Liberator*, at first a very small sheet, the first number of which appeared January 1, 1831. Though small in size, its message to the public was so emphatic morally as to cause it speedily to be heard and felt throughout the country, North and South. It announced the doctrine of immediate, unconditional emancipation as the right of the slave and the duty of the master. Its intrepid editor declared : " I will be as harsh as truth, and as uncompromising as justice. * * * I am in earnest—I will not equivocate—I will not excuse—I will not

retreat a single inch—AND I WILL BE HEARD."
The little paper began without a subscriber;
its editor set the type and did the presswork,
with the aid of a negro boy; lived in his
printing office, and at times subsisted upon a
limited diet of bread and milk. It is said of
John C. Calhoun, of South Carolina, a far-
seeing Southerner, that he remarked, on seeing *The Liberator*, that a spark had been
lighted in Boston, which, if not speedily ex-
tinguished, would ultimately destroy slavery.
The paper was denounced as incendiary;
legislation was proposed to prohibit its circu-
lation in the Southern States; the mails were
searched for it that it might be destroyed;
and the Legislature of Georgia passed a bill,
approved by the Governor, December 26,
1831, offering a reward of $5,000 for the
apprehension and delivery of Mr. Garrison in
that State for summary punishment. Urgent
demands were made upon the mayor and
other citizens of Boston for the suppression of
The Liberator. These finally culminated,
October 21, 1835, in the famous " Boston

mob" of "Gentlemen of property and standing." Mr. Garrison was violently seized by the mob, a rope was placed about his body, and he was dragged through the streets. Finally he was rescued, and lodged in Leverett Street Jail for the preservation of his life. It was this remarkable mob that first arrested the attention of Wendell Phillips, then a young Harvard lawyer, to the anti-slavery movement.

We are, as a people, yet too near the historic anti-slavery conflict for it to be seen generally in its true perspective. It was Garrison who made Lincoln later a possibility. His career is a striking modern illustration of the truth of the declaration : " One shall chase a thousand, and two put ten thousand to flight." His treatment of the question of slavery, so vital to the well-being of the nation, in the sight of the impartial historian of the future, will put to shame the much lauded statesmanship of the Calhouns, Clays, Websters and other eminent Americans of the pro-slavery era.

Returning from my first Boston visit to my

home, in the summer of 1854, I was able, with the help of two or three friends, to arrange, as I had promised, a series of initial anti-slavery meetings, in Columbia County, New York. In one of them I encountered as an opponent a pro-slavery young lawyer from New York. As was the custom in the conduct of such meetings I invited questions and free discussion, a somewhat hazardous experiment, perhaps, for a beginner. At a second meeting in the same locality I was again confronted by this young lawyer, this time re-enforced by one older than himself in experience, Rev. Charles Edwards Lester, who earlier had been an ardent abolitionist, was a delegate to the World's Anti-Slavery Convention in London in 1840, but subsequently became a backslider and a reviler of the abolitionists. At my second meeting, Lester, who chanced to be sojourning in the vicinity and was brought by the young lawyer for the purpose, promptly availed himself of my general invitation and addressed the meeting as an opponent. He ridiculed mercilessly and misrepresented utterly everything I had said, and, in closing, giving me no opportunity for reply, asked the people to leave, saying, " We have been here long enough " ; and himself led the way out of the house. About half of those present followed him, the others remaining to hear what I would say. A friend asked did I know who the speaker was, mentioning his name. It so happened that, though I had never before seen and did not personally know Lester, I had just been reading of his apostacy from the anti-slavery ranks, and of his part in the London World's Anti-Slavery Convention, wherein, in an address, he said, pointing to Mr. Garrison, who was sitting in the gallery, " My friend in the gallery, William Lloyd Garrison, whom I delight to honor !" In my meeting he had denounced Garrison and the abolitionists, as most unworthy, and myself severely for co-operating with them. After turning away from the abolitionists he published a pro-slavery, anti-English volume entitled " The Glory and Shame of England," allied himself with the pro-slavery Democratic party, and, as a reward, obtained a foreign consular appointment. To those who remained of our meeting I gave some account of his checkered career, of which they had not known. A third meeting was then proposed, and a public request made and conveyed to Lester to again attend; but when the time arrived his pro-slavery friends could not persuade him to come, and his statements against Mr. Garrison and the abolitionists were, by his refusal, largely discounted. Of this episode in my initial anti-slavery experience, an account sent to Francis Jackson, whose guest I had been in Boston, was published by Mr. Garrison in *The Liberator*, with a further account of Lester.

To the cold, critical, pro-slavery public, Mr. Garrison was severe and denunciatory. In private, and in the home, he was the most gentle, genial and lovable of men. He had a keen appreciation of the humorous, and was always ready with pleasantry and witticism. He was greatly blessed in the companionship of Mrs. Garrison, who was a woman of rare qualities of mind and heart, and who shared with great heroism and fortitude the privations and perils of the turbulent period of his life. To all who were privileged to enjoy it, and they were many, the hospitality and delightful atmosphere of the Garrison home in Dix Place is a precious memory.

Mr. Garrison was an all-round reformer. As a non-resistant, a friend of peace and the opponent of all war; as an advocate, by precept and example, of temperance; as a broad-minded liberal in religious thought; as the early champion and pioneer of equal rights for woman in all the relations of life; and in later time of the abolition of the white slavery of state regulation of vice and the maintenance of a high, equal standard of morals alike for both men and women, he was as pronounced and as uncompromising as for the abolition of negro slavery. He made most effective use of the Bible in his warfare against slavery. As he would read, from the Old Testament and New, its denunciations of oppression, and of compromise with iniquity, declaring, as in Isaiah, "And your covenant with death shall be disannulled, and your agreement with hell shall not stand," it seemed, indeed, as if, literally, a prophet of the olden time had returned to exhort and admonish a guilty slave-holding people.

He had an abiding faith, exceptionally strong, in immortality and the continued spiritual life. I have before me as I write, among other letters from him, one of deep and tender sympathy, written on the occasion of the death of my youngest brother, Edwin Powell, in 1858, a boy of much promise, in which he writes:

BOSTON, July 25, 1858.

MY DEAR POWELL:

I am made very sad by reading, in the last *Standard*, a notice of the great bereavement which your parents, your sister and yourself have been called to experience, in the removal by death of the dear and noble boy who made your household so bright and full of promise. In every such case "'tis the *survivor* dies." I take it for granted that the departed never have cause to lament their translation; nor would they again return to the earth, in the flesh, if they could; while I am persuaded that our beloved ones, thus removed from our sight, are drawn to us by magnetic affinity, and are more or less frequently by our side, sharing our sorrows and participating in our joys. To me this conviction is very strengthening.

I did not know your stricken brother, but I have no doubt he was a boy of uncommon promise, and that all that is said of him in *The Standard* was justly merited. How loving and promising was my own little boy, Charles Follen, and how suddenly he was taken from me! Having had the same cup of bitterness put to my lips which you are now called upon to drink, I know how to sympathize with you all. Yet I am comforted by the reflection that you need nothing from me to convince you that "it is well with the lad;" that it is a natural event, and neither a dark nor mysterious dispensation; that what is seemingly your loss will be a gain in the end; and that, while the heart may bleed and the tears of affection may fall, a sweet spirit of resignation should be dominant in the heart. * * *

I desire to be most kindly remembered to your parents and sister, proffering to you all my heartfelt sympathies, which are fully shared by my dear wife.

Yours, with the warmest regards,

WM. LLOYD GARRISON.

A. M. POWELL.

He was a delightful traveling companion, as I had occasion to know in attending with him, from time to time, sundry anti-slavery conventions and meetings, and in sharing with him, with others, one or two recreative excursions to the Catskills. In a letter preliminary to one of these mountain excursions, when he would spend a day or two at our rural home in Ghent, he writes:

" Nature now presents her handsomest features and her richest attire. Everything in your region must be looking very attractive: of that I hope to judge in a day or two. But, conceding the fact as settled, I must nevertheless ask, Aaron, ' Did you ever see the Boston Common?' And, if so, ' then I guess you never did see anything like that!'—of course, I mean precisely like it.

"But, 'wind and weather permitting,' we will have a peep together from Bunker Hill[1] at Ghent, and see how the scenery compares with the view from Bunker Hill at Charlestown."

A congratulatory letter upon my approaching marriage, in 1861, in which he had taken a kindly, sympathetic interest, gives a glimpse of him in an aspect little known to the general

[1] A high hill, whose owner's name was Bunker, and commanding an extended, exceptionally beautiful view of the Hudson River Valley and of the Catskill Mountains beyond.

public, to whom he was the critical, severe uncompromising reformer.   He writes :

" I congratulate you both upon your approaching union, and may it prove a perennial fountain of happiness! It seems to have been very early discovered that 'it is not good that the man should be alone;' and yet, in the sequel (if the record may be trusted) it turned out quite the contrary; for he lost Paradise in consequence of eating the forbidden fruit which was offered to him by Eve. Was that 'a help *meet* for him?' In spite of the record, I agree with Milton, or whoever else said it, that woman is 'Heaven's last, best gift to man;' and with Robert Burns, personifying Nature—

> 'Her 'prentice hand she tried on man,
> And then she made the lassies O!'

"By the way, don't you think it was rather sneaking in Adam, after greedily taking his share of the apple, to whiningly plead, by way of self-exculpation, 'The woman whom thou gavest to be with me, she gave me of the tree, and I did eat'? Out upon him! Why didn't he tenderly say 'my wife,' instead of, coldly, 'the woman'? And why didn't he own up, man fashion, and say, like Andrew Jackson, 'I take the responsibility'? He deserved to be expelled from the Garden, anyhow. There are those who would make you and me, in some sense (no! there is no sense in it!) responsible for his shabby conduct at that time! They say he was our 'federal head'; therefore 'in Adam's fall we sinned all'.   I protest against the imputation!"

As a conscientious non-resistant and a lover of peace, the development of the slave-holder's rebellion was in many ways a trying experience for Mr. Garrison, as for Whittier and many other abolitionists opposed to war. But he took a philosophic view of the situation, which is well outlined in a letter which I received from him not long after the firing upon Sumter.   He wrote :

" Technically, the war is to restore the old state of things—fugitive slave law, and all; practically, it is a geographical fight between North and South, and between free and slave institutions. Of the great body of soldiers who have enlisted at the North, comparatively few have any intention or wish to break down the slave system; but God, 'who is above all, and greater than all, and who

'—— moves in a mysterious way
His wonders to perform,'

is making use of them to do 'a strange and terrible work' in righteousness.   I neither deprecate his justice, nor desire to see peace through compromise.   I believe this state of things is hopeful, compared with what it was six months ago."

A very close personal test came to him in the enlistment of his eldest son, George Thompson Garrison, for service in the volunteer army, from truly patriotic considerations, not sharing his father's non-resistant views. He was made a Lieutenant in the 55th Massachusetts colored regiment. As the war advanced, and emancipation was proclaimed, the change of public feeling towards Mr. Garrison was very marked. As I have already mentioned, in connection with the last visit of George Thompson to the United States, both himself and Mr. Garrison were made honored guests of the nation to visit Charleston, S. C., and witness the re-raising of the flag at Sumter, April 14, 1865. Both were given distinguished consideration by President Lincoln and many leading public officials. The restoration of the stars and stripes at Sumter, and the simultaneous surrender of the Southern forces under Lee, to the Northern army under Grant, marked the culmination of the slaveholder's rebellion, and the end, practically, of slavery itself.

The Sumter celebration was, indeed, a most memorable occasion for all who were privileged to share it. Of the Northern visitors, beside those taken South by the steamer *Arago*, as the nation's guests, including Mr. Garrison, George Thompson, Henry Ward Beecher, Rev. Dr. R. S. Storrs, of Brooklyn, still living, Hon. William D. Kelley, of Philadelphia, and others, there was an excursion party of one hundred and eighty-six, mainly from Brooklyn and New York, conveyed by the steamer *Oceanus*, chartered for the occasion. Of this party it was my privilege to be a member, and as a representative of the *New York Tribune*. It included the Rev. Dr. Theodore L. Cuyler, Rev. John W. Chadwick, Hon. Edgar Ketchum, Rev. O. B. Frothingham, Rev. A. P. Putnam, Joshua Leavitt, and others. General Stewart L. Woodford, then a Colonel, and chief of Major-General Gillmore's Staff, (and our late United States Minister at Madrid, at the outbreak of the war with Spain,) was in charge of the details of the celebration. The day was clear and beautiful, the several steamers, including the *Oceanus*, conveying representatives of the army and navy, guests, and visitors from Charleston to the historic Fort Sumter, were gaily decorated for the occasion. Precisely at noon Major-General Robert Anderson took the same flag which four years before he had been compelled to lower, and, assisted by many others, raised it to the top of the staff from which it was again unfurled to the breeze and greeted with great enthusiasm. Henry Ward Beecher then gave an address, characteristic, eloquent, and spoken with deep feeling, and published in full in the reconstructed *Charleston Courier*, of April 15, 1865, a copy of which lies before me as I write. To the deserted office of this journal, once a very zealous defender of slavery and violent advocate of secession, then in charge of Northern men, Mr. Garrison paid a visit after the celebration at Sumter, and with his own practiced hands set up a paragraph of Henry Ward Beecher's memorable address! The following day an immense meeting, attended by three or four thousand, mainly freed men and women, was held in the very large "Zion's Church," used as a place of worship by the colored people. It was at first intended to hold an out-of-doors meeting, in Citadel Square, where a speakers' platform had been erected. A great crowd of freed people gathered, and Mr. Garrison's presence becoming known, he was greeted with wild enthusiasm, lifted to the shoulders of men who carried him triumphantly to the platform. The meeting was adjourned to the church on account of Senator Wilson, of Massachusetts, —afterward Vice President—who was also to address it, but could not prudently speak in the open air. Major-General Rufus Saxton presided, and beside the addresses of Mr. Garrison and Senator Wilson, George Thompson also spoke, and all were greeted with unbounded enthusiasm by the eager multitude.

Another memorable and most impressive incident of the Charleston experience was a visit by Mr. Garrison, accompanied by Senator Wilson, Hon. Edgar Ketchum and others, to the camp of the 55th Massachusetts Regiment, located about three miles from the city, where Lieutenant George Thompson Garrison had, with his company, a short time previous to our arrival at the camp, brought in from the deserted plantations of the interior twelve hundred abandoned slaves, "contrabands," as they were then called. They were a ragged, most forlorn looking company of greatly impoverished, ignorant men, women and children, a striking object lesson of the misery and degradation begotten by slavery! The meeting and embrace of father and son under such circumstances, and with such an environment, was impressive, quite beyond the power of words to describe! The poor creatures, ignorant as they were, seemed intuitively drawn to Mr. Garrison as their friend and deliverer. It was most pathetic to see them gather about him, and, approaching timidly, touch his garments. As a picture, photographed upon my brain more than thirty years ago, it is still vivid in memory and will be indelible. It was a scene which some competent artist should have commemorated upon canvas in a great historic painting!

On the return voyage of the *Oceanus* we learned, from a signal message given us by a south-bound steamer, of the assassination of President Lincoln! We returned, with sorrow and solicitude, direct to New York, without stopping, as we had intended, at Fortress Monroe and Washington.

With the adoption and ratification of the Thirteenth Amendment of the Constitution of the United States, abolishing slavery, in the judgment of Mr. Garrison, the time had arrived to discontinue the American Anti-Slavery Society, and to rely upon other agencies for securing negro enfranchisement. At this juncture differences of opinion developed between himself and Mr. Phillips. These were shared by others, long time friends of, and co-workers with, each. They were, essentially, differences of method rather than of fundamental principle. Mr. Garrison discontinued *The Liberator*, December 29,

1865. The American Anti-Slavery Society was continued, with Mr. Phillips as President, until April 16, 1870, till the ratification of a Fifteenth Amendment, which secured, legally, the equal enfranchisement of colored men as citizens. Mr. Garrison, through the press and upon the platform, continued individually and independently, though in sympathetic relations with the Republican party, faithfully to exert an important, helpful national influence in behalf of humane, just treatment for the colored people, and their actual, as well as legal, enfranchisement upon equal terms with the whites.

I have myself always regretted that it had not been possible to continue indefinitely, in some form, a nucleus of the American Anti-Slavery Society, with its funded moral capital, to be, in the United States, the counterpart, and something more, of the British and Foreign Anti-Slavery Society of Great Britain. If only an Independent Committee of competent men and women, kept wholly distinct from all partisan political alliances, and thereby

free from the suspicion of selfish party political ends, its effective moral censorship of
public men and measures, especially as involving the rights of the colored people, would
even now, thirty years after emancipation, be
most valuable and timely, in view of the
monstrous outrages to which, as in the Caro-
linas, Louisiana and elsewhere, they have
been, in the long interim, and yet are, subjected.

While, as I have previously mentioned,
Mr. Garrison was interested in, and helpful to,
many reforms, his greatest service, apart from
his anti-slavery career, which was pre-eminent,
was undoubtedly to the cause of equal rights
for women, in all the relations of life. A
signal illustration of this quite ante-dates the
modern woman movement, which now as-
sumes important proportions, and, indeed,
may be said to have had much to do with
its inauguration. It is his part, heroic and
unprecedented in self sacrifice, in connection
with the World's Anti-Slavery Convention in
London in 1840. It was a crucial time in

JOSEPHINE E. BUTLER.

the anti-slavery reform, of which he was the acknowledged American leader. The delegates from this country included several women, Lucretia Mott and others, and when they reached London, though they had journeyed three thousand miles to attend it, because they were women they were not allowed seats in the convention. Mr. Garrison, going by a later vessel, was delayed on the ocean and did not arrive until after action had been taken by the convention refusing to seat, as members, the American women delegates. Upon learning of this unjust, illiberal action Mr. Garrison declined a seat in the convention, and instead sat with the rejected women in the gallery. He has many times since spoken earnestly and effectively in behalf of women, but this was, indeed, heroic action, the wide spread, far reaching influence of which, under the exceptional circumstances, no eloquence of speech could parallel.

To Josephine E. Butler and other of our European co-workers for the abolition of State regulation of vice, which not inappropriately they designate as the "New Abolitionist Movement," Mr. Garrison's example as an American Abolitionist, as I have had occasion to know, has been a constant source of inspiration and strength. In 1876, when Rev. J. P. Gledstone and Henry J. Wilson, M.P., visited this country as a deputation from the International Federation, he welcomed them cordially to Boston, and became one of a committee of vigilance for that city, with Wendell Phillips, Lucy Stone and others, to resist the threatened encroachments of the American regulation propagandists.

In May, 1877, I received from him a letter, written just on the eve of his sailing for his last visit in England, a facsimile of which is reproduced on the following page.

During this last visit in England, in 1877, he visited Mrs. Butler at her home, and spoke in sundry private and public gatherings in Liverpool, London, Birmingham and elsewhere, greatly to the comfort and encouragement of our English "New Abolitionist" friends. On his return to this country, The

New York, May 22, 1877.

Dear friend Powell:

Accept my thanks for your paper on "State Regulation of Vice," in pamphlet form, which I hope will be seen and read by many. The subject discussed is one that challenges universal attention, as it relates to habits, usages, and legal sanctions of immorality, which are sapping the foundations of society on both sides of the ~~country~~ Atlantic, especially in Great Britain and on the Continent.

To-morrow I embark in the Algeria for Liverpool, where I hope to meet the devoted Mrs. Butler and other noble co-workers in the cause of purity.

Yours for the holy conflict,

Wm. Lloyd Garrison.

New York Committee for the Prevention of State Regulation of Vice, now The American Purity Alliance, in January, 1878, gave him a reception in the parlors of the "Isaac T. Hopper Home," on which occasion he made an address which strongly reminded many who listened to it of his most eloquent, uncompromising anti-slavery addresses of an earlier period.   In January of the year following, 1879, the year of his death, in response to an invitation to attend and address the Annual Meeting and Subscription Anniversary of our New York Committee, I received from him the following earnest, characteristic letter :

Boston, Jan. 14, 1879.

My Dear Friend:

I wish it were in my power to be one of the company that will assemble to-morrow evening at the Isaac T. Hopper Home, with reference to the Subscription Anniversary in aid of the New York Committee for the Prevention of State Regulated Vice; but I can only send you this hastily written note, in which to express the deep interest I feel in the object sought to be accomplished, and my high appreciation of the efforts made so earnestly and untiringly by you and your estimable associates to that end. That constant vigilance is needed to prevent the adoption in this country of a system of licensed prostitution, similar to that which obtains on the other side of the Atlantic under the mask of a beneficent sanitary regulation, is certain; and that, thus far, the attempts made in various quarters to secure this profligate legislation have been frustrated to a large extent by the timely warnings, the solemn appeals, and the faithful testimonies scattered widely through your associated action, admits of no question. Hence you well deserve the countenance and helping hand of the truly pure and good in the community, that your labors may be continued, your means of enlightening and guiding public sentiment enhanced, and your members greatly multiplied.

You will not fail to bear in remembrance the tremendous struggle that is going on in Great Britain between the upholders and the opponents of the so called " Contagious Diseases Acts," nor to send to the latter the strongest words of encouragement; for the world has never before seen such a morally sublime uprising against statutory licentiousness, and for the preservation of personal chastity and public virtue. In some of its aspects it closely resembles the conflict that was so hotly waged in this country for the abolition of chattel slavery; and we know what that required of ardent consecration, noble self sacrifice and unfaltering trust in God. * * Truly yours,

WM. LLOYD GARRISON.

AARON M. POWELL.

His death occurred in New York the following May. It called forth from all parts of the country, many expressions of profound respect and esteem.

Our New York Committee, Abby Hopper Gibbons in the chair, adopted the following:

Resolved, That it is with deep regret and a profound consciousness of our great loss, that we record the death of William Lloyd Garrison; that, prophetic, fearless and uncompromising as the champion of and deliverer of the negro slave, so was he foremost among his countrymen as an outspoken antagonist of the enslavement of women and degradation of men, involved in licensed, or "regulated" prostitution; that we commend to all the lesson of unswerving fidelity to convictions of duty and the right, taught by his rare example; and that we hereby express to his children our heartfelt sympathy in their great bereavement,—our joy in their rich legacy of his loving and precious memory.

Boston, through whose streets he had been dragged by a furious mob, with a rope about his body at the peril of his life, and again wherein a threatening gallows had been erected in front of his dwelling, has since honored itself, in fitly honoring his memory, by placing a finely executed, life-like bronze statue of him in Commonwealth Avenue, one of its most popular thoroughfares.

CHAPTER III.

——

On my first journey to Western New York for my initial meetings as Lecturing Agent of the American Anti-Slavery Society, in September, 1854, I had as my traveling companion from Albany to Syracuse, Francis Jackson, of Boston. He was en route to Syracuse to attend a semi-annual meeting of the American Anti-Slavery Society, which I also attended.

It was Francis Jackson, one of the "solid men" of Boston, who, when the mob of 1835 broke up the annual meeting of the Boston Female Anti-Slavery Society, and drove its members from their hall, opened his own house for their meeting, and, in most vigorous and uncompromising terms, publicly espoused the cause of the enslaved and defended the right of free speech. His home, to which I was most kindly welcomed on my first visit to Boston, as subsequently until his death, was

REV. SAMUEL J. MAY.

in Hollis street, not far from Mr. Garrison's in Dix Place. His cordial welcome to me, with his fatherly interest and encouragement, is a most pleasant memory of my early anti-slavery experience.

At the Syracuse meetings I also met Rev. Samuel J. May, who was one of Mr. Garrison's earliest coadjutors, and whom to know was to love. Genial and gentle, he was also morally heroic, and ready to brave any amount of opposition and persecution, of which he had much, for the sake of what he believed to be right. As an Anti-Slavery Secretary, in earlier years, and in his efforts in behalf of Prudence Crandall, a cultivated young Quaker woman, who was outrageously persecuted on account of having proposed to teach colored girls in her private school in Canterbury, Conn.,—a well nigh incredible manifestation of the pro-slavery, negro-hating spirit of the time, he exhibited the highest order of manly heroism and moral courage. In my later anti-slavery labors it was my privilege not infrequently to attend anti-slavery meetings and conventions with him, and always with a feeling of gratitude for his delightful companionship.

At this Syracuse semi-annual meeting of 1854 Mr. Garrison also was present and presided. The secretaries appointed for the occasion were John C. Hanchett, of Syracuse, Susan B. Anthony, of Rochester, and myself; its Business Committee was composed of Mr. May, Lucy Stone, Charles Lenox Remond, Lydia Mott, of Albany, and Rev. Andrew T. Foss, of New Hampshire ; and there were also among the speakers, Rev. Beriah Green, Gerrit Smith, Frederick Douglass, William Wells Brown, Hon. Leonard Gibbs, and others less widely known as abolitionists. It was an inspiring meeting, especially for one just entering upon active anti-slavery service, as was I at that time. Held in connection with, or immediately following it, was also a very enthusiastic " Jerry Rescue " meeting, to commemorate the rescue of a fugitive slave named Jerry, three years previous, October 1, 1852, from the minions of the odious Fugitive Slave Law, by whom he had been seized in Syracuse with the purpose of returning him to slavery.

It was in January, 1861, half a dozen years later, after the election of Lincoln, but before his inauguration as President of the United States, that I was again in Syracuse to attend an anti-slavery convention, under the auspices of the American Anti-Slavery Society, the preliminary arrangements for which had been made by Mr. May. The other speakers for this occasion were Rev. Beriah Green, Susan B. Anthony and Charles D. B. Mills, besides Mr. May and myself. On going to the hall at the appointed time we found it filled with an unruly mob, convened for the purpose of preventing the holding of our convention. When Mr. May attempted to remonstrate, he was immediately threatened with personal violence by ruffians who surrounded him, and like violent treatment was extended to the late Rev. M. E. Strieby, D. D., who was then a Congregational minister in Syracuse.

It being found impossible to hold our convention in the hall as advertised, a well known and much respected physician, Dr. R. W. Pease, kindly offered his house for the purpose, and a session was held therein at which several addresses were delivered and a series of appropriate resolutions adopted, which appeared in the newspapers of the following day. Some of the citizens of Syracuse, indignant at this mobocratic interference with free speech in their city, called a public meeting for the following day, to be held in the same hall, to protest against the action of the mob, and to test the faithfulness of the city authorities. Some of the anti-slavery speakers who had been denied a hearing the day before were invited also to speak. At this "free speech" citizens' meeting, Rev. Dr. Strieby was called to the chair. The hall was crowded, many "Jerry Rescuers" being present, determined to vindicate the right of free speech, and many also of the mob of the day previous. Dr. Strieby was listened to quietly during his opening address. At its close, as I happened to be sitting very near him, and was most available, he called upon me, as one who was to have addressed the convention, the day before, to speak. The moment I began to address the meeting the mobocrats commenced to howl, and continued a great noise. Then the chairman asked me to suspend, but not to resume my seat, and he made another appeal for free speech, which was quietly listened to as before. When he asked me again to proceed with my remarks the mob began immediately to howl vociferously. This was several times repeated, he being listened to quietly and I retaining the platform at his request, at once interrupted with much noise, until the confusion became very great. When, finally, the rioters began to press forward toward the platform, a group of excited " Jerry Rescuers " gathered in front and a collision seemed imminent. As one threw himself partly on the platform at my feet, and at the same moment, putting his hand in his side pocket, grasped his revolver, Dr. Strieby turned to me and said that he thought we had done all we reasonably could do to secure the object of the meeting, and suggested that I, and my associates of the anti-slavery speakers, should retire from the hall. We were conducted quietly and unobserved by a rear passage to the street, leaving the mob in possession as on the previous day. In the evening they celebrated their victory over the abolitionists by a parade, led by a band of music, with transparencies bearing these inscriptions: " Freedom of Speech, but not Treason ;" " The Rights of the South must be protected;" " Abolitionism no longer in Syracuse;" " The Jerry Rescuers played out." Two large sized effigies were carried in the procession, one of a man, the other of a woman, bearing the names respectively of Mr. May and Miss Anthony, and these, after the parade through some of the principal streets of the city, were taken to Hanover Square, and there burned amid shouts, hootings, profanity and shameful ribaldry !

From Syracuse I journeyed for my first

lecture appointments to Ontario County, the village of Naples, and in adjoining towns, appointments which were kindly made for me by relatives and friends residing in the vicinity. Naples was the home of Hon. Myron H. Clark, who was then the Whig and Temperance candidate for Governor, and subsequently elected at that autumnal election. With the sensitiveness everywhere prevalent at that time on the subject of slavery, my meetings, even in the smaller towns and villages, were not infrequently exciting and controversial. I recall one instance, in Rushford, Alleghany County, where our meeting began at seven in the evening and was continued till nearly two o'clock in the morning! My statements concerning the prevalent ecclesiastical complicity with slavery were challenged by two ministers who were present, one Baptist, the other Methodist, who appeared as zealous defenders of their respective churches. Others joined in the discussion, pro and con, thus prolonging the meeting till the early hours of the morning. The experiences of the anti-slavery lecturer of that period were varied and sometimes unique in private contact with the people, as well as in meetings. The entertainment, generally in private homes, was of all sorts, sometimes very enjoyable and restful; frequently quite otherwise. With the pro-slavery prejudice and consequent antagonism everywhere encountered, with the irregular hours of sleeping and eating, it is, as I write at this distance of time, somewhat with a feeling of surprise that I survived it all!

At the conclusion of this first series of meetings in Ontario, Alleghany and Cattaraugus Counties, I visited Rochester, where I was very kindly welcomed as a guest of relatives then residing there, and by a group of anti-slavery friends. The Rochester visit at that time was also made memorable by the opportunity it gave me to hear for the first time, on the lyceum platform, Wendell Phillips, and to meet and counsel with him concerning my anti-slavery work.

Wendell Phillips

WENDELL PHILLIPS.

In every generation are a few great men. In America's group of the present century is Wendell Phillips. Without official position, always in the minority, the champion of the weak against the strong, he made himself heard and felt, in his own and in other lands, as few, under kindred conditions, have ever done. By the inherent force of brilliant intellect, of a keen sense of justice, and the rarest of oratorical gifts, he became a master among masters, a leader of leaders.

He was born in Boston, November 29, 1811. His father, John Phillips, was first Mayor of Boston, for several years President of the Massachusetts Senate, a man of wealth and high social position, a descendant of Rev. George Phillips, a Puritan, and first minister of Watertown, Mass. Mr. Phillips' boyhood was spent in the Boston Latin School; he entered Harvard College before he was sixteen, and graduated before he was twenty. In view of his subsequent career, it is a curious fact that he was a leader of the aristocratic party in the University, President of an ex-clusive Society, known as the "Gentlemen's Club." He used to say that to himself be-longed the "infamy" of having defeated the first proposition to organize a Temperance Society in Harvard College! He was a rapid learner, and stood high in his class, was deeply interested in history and chemistry, and had a passion for mechanics. "If I had followed my own bent," he said, "I would have given my time to mechanics or chemistry;"—adding : "My mother used to say that when I became a lawyer, a good carpenter was spoiled!"

Sumner and Motley were his college mates and lifelong friends. He graduated from the Cambridge Law School in 1833, and was admitted to the bar in 1834. In his college life he was partial to the Debating Club, but had not then become interested in the anti-slavery movement. He had just entered upon the practice of law, and it was upon leaving his office on the memorable afternoon of the Boston Mob of October 21, 1835, when Mr. Garrison was dragged through the streets, that his attention was first seriously called to the anti-slavery movement. He had then no anti-slavery interest, but was "indignant on the ground of fair play." It was his wife, he says, who the next year made him an abolitionist. He joined the American Anti-Slavery Society in 1836. The year following, November 7, 1837, occurred the murder of Rev. Elijah P. Lovejoy, and the wanton destruction of his anti-slavery printing press by a pro-slavery mob at Alton, Illinois. This shocking outrage in the interest of slavery moved Dr. Channing and others to petition the Mayor and Aldermen of Boston for the use of Faneuil Hall, the old "Cradle of Liberty," for a public indignation meeting. The petition was first refused and afterward granted. It was at this meeting, held December 8, 1837, that Mr. Phillips made his first great speech, which won for him at once an acknowledged place in the front rank of conspicuous orators. The Attorney-General of Massachusetts, James T. Austin, had made a bitter pro-slavery speech, declaring Lovejoy "presumptuous and impudent," that he " died as the fool dieth," etc. His speech caused great excitement in the meeting. Mr. Phillips, who was present but not intending to speak, was much stirred. Though young and unknown, he presently made himself heard above the tumult. Referring to the Attorney-General's speech, he declared :

" Sir, when I heard the gentleman lay down principles which place the murderers of Alton side by side with Otis and Hancock, with Quincy and Adams, I thought those pictured lips, [pointing to the portraits in the historic hall,] would have broken into voice to rebuke the recreant American—the slanderer of the dead ! "

Great applause, and counter applause followed, and again he said :

" Sir, for the sentiments he has uttered, on soil consecrated by the prayers of Puritans, and the blood of patriots, the earth should have yawned and swallowed him up ! " Then followed applause, hisses, and a great outcry: "Take that back ! " There was great confusion, and finally, resuming, Mr. Phillips, said: "I cannot take back my words," and proceeded with his masterly, eloquent reply, declaring, "When Liberty is in danger, Faneuil Hall has the right, it is her duty to strike the key-note for the United States!" His speech turned the tide, and anti-slavery and free speech resolutions were triumphantly adopted.

His eloquent advocacy was, indeed, a great accession for the anti-slavery reform. For himself was involved the sacrifice of brilliant professional prospects, social position, family and other cherished friendships—all on the altar of the slave !

His wife, Ann Greene Phillips, was a woman of rare moral discernment and great force of character. Though an invalid during most of their married life, she entered most heartily into his varied experiences of sacrifice and triumph, and exhorted him to continued and uncompromising steadfastness at whatever cost. Together they attended the World's Anti-Slavery Convention in London in 1840, and afterward visited the Continent. In that Convention Mr. Phillips exhausted every resource within his power to secure the admission and proper recognition of the American women delegates. The bigoted conservatism of the convention was, however, more than a match for even his eloquent and resourceful advocacy.

When in Edinburgh, Scotland, the guest of Elizabeth Pease Nichol, in her hospitable home, Huntley Lodge, I was shown a strikingly beautiful portrait of Mr. Phillips, as a young man, painted for Mrs. Nichol, by the artist, Haydon, at the time of the World's Anti-Slavery Convention. His features are also readily recognizable in the large historic picture, by Haydon, with many of the delegates and visitors to the convention, which is now in the National Gallery, London.

Mr. Phillips, like Mr. Garrison and the abolitionists in general, was often complained of on account of the harshness of his criticism and the severity of his denunciation. Asking "What is the denunciation with which we are charged?" he answers, " It is endeavoring, in our faltering human speech, to declare the enormity of making merchandise of men,—of separating husband and wife,—taking the infant from the mother, and selling the daughter to prostitution,—of a professedly Christian nation denying, by statute, the Bible to every sixth man and woman of its population, and making it illegal for two or three to meet together, except a white man be present!"

After the culmination of the great anti-slavery conflict Mr. Phillips said to a friend: " I never yet had, toward any man whom I criticised, the slightest unkind feeling. I criticised them always from a moral stand-point, and as sinners against a race or a principle."

In a prolonged period of familiar intercourse I can say of him, that in private I never knew him to personally criticise anyone unkindly or harshly.

He was pre-eminently the orator of the anti-slavery movement. In the rarest gifts and graces of oratory he was without a peer on either side of the Atlantic. It has been my privilege in England to listen to Mr. Gladstone, John Bright, Lord Rosebery, Lord Salisbury, the present Premier; the Duke of Devonshire, the Unionist leader; John Morley and other representative English public men, but in oratory Mr. Phillips was quite superior to either of them. Emerson says: "There is no true eloquence unless there is a man behind the speech." In Mr. Phillips' case true manliness, in the highest sense, gave a mighty impetus to his eloquent voice. His training, as he explained it, was chiefly in the school of the anti-slavery agitation,—believing what he advocated, and an intense desire to persuade others.

He was most kindly and helpful with young people, encouraging on their part, in quiet ways, aspirations for useful service. Very grateful to me is the memory of his sympathetic counsel as I met him, by appointment, for a quiet interview, at his hotel in Rochester, concerning my own anti-slavery labors in connection with the American Anti-Slavery

Society.   Among other practical suggestions which he then made concerning public speaking, was to cultivate the habit of writing, as a mental discipline.   " Write something," he said, " every day of your life ; write, but do not read."   He added, " write to the *Anti-Slavery Standard*,"—and in accordance with his suggestion, I began soon after, an occasional correspondence with that journal.   Later I received from him a letter of counsel and suggestion concerning public speaking which I valued highly, and have treasured during the intervening years.   It accompanied an interesting little volume, to which it refers, entitled, " Hints on Public Speaking."   I present the letter herewith as follows :

Feb'y, '60.

DEAR FRIEND:

I mail you to-day the little book I spoke of, with trembling though on this account.

I recognize the use of preparation, full and careful, also how much we owe the slave to serve him the *best* we can; and yet again how much the field has changed since I entered.   *Now* with the press crowded and every rostrum, pro and con, on slavery, it is a hard task to interest an audience; *once* the feeblest voice on the right side was useful and potent.

Still I remember that in the beginning we never thought, much less talked, whether such a one had made a good speech. We just obeyed an irrepressible impulse, rushed into the fight and struck the best blow we could, and never thought whether it was scientifically done. That hot, unconscious earnestness has made us what we all are. Try to save it and add what skill you can by study. Be filled with a devoted love of our cause, so full as to be insensible to the opinions of others; and except now and then, in serious wish to improve, discourage criticism on each other's merits and manner; it chills the ardor and vitiates the sacrifice.

There are good hints in this book with some serious errors.

Good-by.

Yours faithfully,

WENDELL PHILLIPS.

A. M. POWELL.

Mr. Phillips placed great value upon the Lyceum as a popular, educational force. He was himself, of course, a great favorite upon its platform. Even pro-slavery Lyceum managers made many demands upon him, especially for his celebrated lecture, which gave pleasure to so many, and which he was so often called upon to deliver after it had been widely published, the "Lost Arts." He used sometime to write to the managers that he would give them his "Lost Arts," or "Street Life in Europe," also a great favorite with Lyceum patrons, for $100 or $200, as the case might be; but, if they would allow it, he would come for an anti-slavery lecture free, and pay his own expenses! He would frequently give an extended anti-slavery prelude to his Lyceum audiences, which he humorously called the "portico" to his lecture! His lectures abounded in humorous surprises, of which a good illustration, in the "Lost Arts," was his description of the ancient Damascus blade of flexible steel, "so fine that it could be put into a scabbard like a corkscrew, and bent every way without breaking—like an American politician!"

Master as he was on the platform, he was never wholly free from a sensitive feeling in approaching it, which in others sometimes developes into stage fright. He once said to me as I was walking with him in Albany from his hotel to the hall wherein a great lecture audience awaited his coming: "I never ascend the platform without a feeling of weakness in my knees!"

His own tribute to O'Connell, wherein he said, "Broadly considered, his eloquence has never been equalled in modern times, certainly not in English speech," was quite as appropriate to himself.

He was much occupied in thought with grave topics, but he had much quiet humor, and in private, as those who stood near him well know, was a delightful companion.

In his boyhood he conceived a strong prejudice against Quakers, to which he sometimes playfully referred in conversation with myself and others of his anti-slavery friends who were associated with the Society of Friends. It appears that at the close of a summer in the family cottage at Nahant, by the sea, it was decided that the cottage needed painting in its interior, and the father said, "There is so and so, an honest Lynn Quaker, we will leave the keys with him and have him do the painting, and it will be all in good order for us when we come again next summer." But, unfortunately, there was some slip in the quality of the paint which the Lynn Quaker had used, and when they next opened their cottage the following summer all the chairs stuck to the floor! This experience, Mr. Phillips said, gave him, as a boy, a strong bias against the Quakers! He was present on one occasion at a meeting of the Chestnut Street Club, Boston, at which I was invited to read a paper on " The Lesson of Quakerism," and shared in the discussion which followed. Half playfully he made some critical comments upon Friends, which were well understood and enjoyed by those present. As reported by a correspondent, and subsequently published in the *Anti-Slavery Standard*, they had a more serious look, and were not as readily understood, and were followed by many letters of earnest protest to Mr. Phillips from Friends in Pennsylvania and elsewhere, his personal friends, who were among *The Standard's* readers!

He was an eloquent, influential pioneer advocate of equal rights for women, as well as of the slave's emancipation. He had championed the rights of women in the World's Anti-Slavery Convention of 1840, and in the controversy of that period which had resulted in a division among American Abolitionists. He was one of the speakers at the Worcester Woman's Rights Convention in 1851, which gave a powerful impetus to the initial agitation for equality of rights, civil and political, for American women.   In his masterly address on that occasion he spoke of the movement as "The first organized protest against the injustice which has brooded over the character and destiny of one-half of the human race," and as "The most magnificent reform that has yet been launched upon the world."   One who was present says that the effect was very marked in the convention, when, at one point in his memorable address, he was interrupted with hisses, he said : " There are two kinds of

creatures that hiss—serpents and geese"—
and he hoped there were none of these in the
convention! There was no more hissing.

Before Legislative Committees and upon
Lyceum and other platforms, he made many
eloquent pleas in behalf of justice for women.
His last public address, in the Old South
Church, Boston, was upon this theme, on the
occasion of the unveiling of a statue commem-
orative of Harriet Martineau.

He was a deeply interested, influential
advocate of the cause of Temperance, with
which he was wont to deal as a question of
statesmanship, involving the perpetuity of the
Republic. He used to say: "The Tories of
Europe look across the Atlantic and ask us to
show them a well governed city and we cannot
do it." He was, of course, a total abstainer,
and the influence of his example in this particular was on one occasion exemplified in
connection with an informal dinner given by
Mr. Sumner to himself and Mr. Motley on the
occasion of the latter's return from Europe.
Mr. Motley was accustomed to wine, as was

Mr. Sumner himself. Mr. Sumner wished to be equally courteous to both his guests. In his dilemma he conferred, with some solicitude, with a friend of mine as to what he should do. It was finally arranged that a bottle of wine should be placed upon the table for Mr. Motley and at the proper time Mr. Sumner would say : " Motley, help yourself to wine ;" he would, of course, offer none to Mr. Phillips, nor would he take any himself. The dinner passed off pleasantly, Mr. Phillips meanwhile being wholly unconscious of the solicitude Mr. Sumner had had on account of his teetotal principles!

His sympathy for the wronged and oppressed extended also to the Indians, the Chinese and the Irish, as well as to the enslaved colored people. " Every American," he declared, referring to broken treaties, "ought to blush at this nation's treatment of the Indians." He said: " Make them citizens; hold them responsible to our civil law; secure them its protection; call home the cheats and cutthroats who only exasperate and abuse them.   Do justice if you expect to receive it. Show them civilization before you expect them to enjoy it."

He was a philanthropist of the widest scope. He had a deep interest in prison reform; was strongly opposed to the death penalty; was much stirred by the sometimes cruel treatment of the insane; and earnestly advocated fewer hours of labor, better educational advantages, and greater political independence, for the laboring classes.   After his retirement from lecturing he was much occupied with these varied philanthropic and humane interests. In a letter received from him in this period he writes me: " I have done with lecturing,—am a man of leisure,—except that I never have a minute to spare."   His last letter was on behalf of a man wrongly imprisoned in Worcester, and on the day of his death he was to have made an appeal for him in a Worcester court.

He deprecated the modern growth of great corporations and the gigantic combinations of capital, especially as a controlling force in legislation, and, referring to the then masterful President of the Pennsylvania Railroad, was wont to say: "Scott, of Harrisburg, has $450,000,000 under his hands, and as he moves from San Francisco to his Eastern lunching place every sweep of his garments knocks down a Legislature!"

He was a profound believer in agitation, defined by Sir Robert Peel as "the marshalling of the conscience of a nation to mould its laws." Mr. Phillips said of it that it is: "The method that puts the school by the side of the ballot box. Agitation prevents rebellions, keeps the peace and secures progress. Muskets are the weapons of animals. Agitation is the atmosphere of brains."

His last great address, the greatest of his life, was at the centennial anniversary of the Phi Beta Kappa of Harvard College in June 1881. Harvard's most brilliant orator, he had been many times invited, but always hitherto with limitations which he declined to accept. On this occasion he was left wholly free. He chose for his theme, "The Scholar in a

Republic." He interpreted fearlessly and eloquently, to a very distinguished assemblage of scholars, the duty and responsibility of scholarship; arraigned its timidity; and summoned its representatives to the championship of liberty, justice and needed reforms. I quote from the conclusion of his address the following:

" To be as good as our fathers we must be better. They silenced their fears and subdued their prejudices, inaugurating free speech and equality with no precedent on the file. Europe shouted ' Madmen,' and gave us forty years for the shipwreck. With serene faith they persevered. Let us rise to their level. Crush appetite and prohibit temptation if it rots great cities. Intrench labor in sufficient bulwark against that wealth which, without the tenfold strength of modern incorporation, wrecked the Grecian and Roman States ; and, with a sterner effort still, summon women into civil life as re-enforcement to our laboring ranks in the effort to make our civilization a success.

" Sit not, like the figure on our silver coin, looking ever backward."

In a message I received from him accompanying a copy of the address soon after its delivery, he wrote : " I thought they might

hiss me.   But they showed their true education by bearing it well.   Indeed I seldom
have had such cheers, and such a warm
reception."

He was tenderly sympathetic, as only those
who stood nearest him knew.   On the occasion of parting with our beloved daughter, a
lovely little girl in her fourth year, in December, 1867, he wrote:

"I know how weak all words are to comfort you
for such a loss.   Be sure our hearts go out to you
in loving and tenderest sympathy.   God give you
all consolation and hold up your hearts.   These
dear little pets twine round our hearts so closely, it
is such agony to part with them.   But such part-
ings wean us, as we need to be, from these scenes,
putting our treasures on the other side.   How
near, real and dear that world becomes after these
transfers!

"Tell your wife how fully we feel with her,
sorrowing with you both in this great sorrow.   But
this dear blessing, lent for a little while, is not taken
away—only lifted that you may more easily look up
to it."

Again, ten years later, February, 1877,
following the death of my mother he wrote:

"Your wife writes me of your mother's death. We sympathize most tenderly with you. I know how sad it is parting with a mother—nothing like it in the rest of life. Long years ago I passed through that experience, and the feeling of loneliness—of the loss of something to be sheltered under —is still fresh. I wonder if other grown men feel this as keenly as I did at thirty. You have been so happy in having your parents live so far into your life. I cannot imagine anything sweeter than seeing one's reward in their satisfaction and whatever repute we gain gladden their eyes.

"How well I remember that circle of earnest and thoughtful workers I used to meet at Hudson— trained, far sighted and devoted. One could see the rich soil in which your life had its roots. No blessing greater than such a cradle. To such death is only a step upward to broader fields of labor. When it comes in fulness of years we only sorrow for it for our loss. The blessing of interest, like ours, in great ideas seems to me to be that even death seems hardly a separation. * * My wife sends you both her tenderest love."

Rarely beautiful was his loving devotion to his fondly cherished, long suffering, invalid wife, to the nursing of whom, in her great helplessness, much of his time was given during the last years of his life. His very earnest desire was that he might outlive her, and so be able to minister affectionately to her needs to the end. Near his last moments, when the time of parting was at hand, his last words were: "I am willing to die to-day as well as at any time—but for my poor wife— I had hoped I should have outlived her."

He was a thorough Bostonian, fond of his native city. In an important anti-slavery crisis he said:

"I love inexpressibly these streets of Boston over whose pavements my mother held up tenderly my baby feet, and, if God permits me time enough, I will make them too pure to bear the footsteps of a slave."

During my several visits to Europe, in meeting with the "New Abolitionists" of the Old World, Mrs. Josephine Butler and others, I have been much impressed with the marked influence of his life and teaching in connection with their great conflict with a gigantic iniquity. He expressed much interest in, and sympathy with, my second European visit in 1877, when I went especially to attend the first International Congress, held in Geneva, Switzerland, at which was organized the International Federation for the Abolition of State Regulation of Vice. With a message of love, of which he commissioned me to be the bearer to Mrs. Butler and others, he kindly sent to me a general "credential," which I found especially helpful on various occasions. A facsimile I present on the following page.

He gave me a special letter to Thomas Hughes, "Tom Brown of Rugby," then a member of the House of Commons, which was honored in a most hearty manner, and opened for me at the time a door of rich opportunity for contact with, and the study of, sundry representative, distinguished English public men, and the numerous associations, of greatest interest, which cluster about the historic Parliament Buildings.

Mr. and Mrs. Phillips' home life was of exceptional simplicity and plainness. Their Essex Street house, which they occupied for so many years, until finally driven from it, after a long period of waiting, by the city

Boston, U.S.A.
27th August, 1877

My friend, Mr
Aaron M. Powell,
of New York, visits
Europe to attend
Reform Conventions

in Geneva & Glasgow.

He is so devoted,
efficient & widely known
a worker on all, our
Reform questions, and
specially Peace,
Temperance; Negro
emancipation and
Justice to Women,
as to need no
introduction or

indorsement, in America.

But, if my name
can aid him any where
I commend him most
heartily to the kindness
& confidence of all
who are at work
to help human progress
Wendell Phillips

authorities, for a street improvement, was very plain and unpretentious, and in this respect a surprise, especially, to foreign visitors. This locality, become historic, is now marked by a memorial tablet to Mr. Phillips, placed on a house, which occupies in part the site of his former Essex Street home, by the City of Boston. It bears the following inscription :

"Here Wendell Phillips resided during forty years, devoted by him to efforts to secure the abolition of African slavery in this country. The charms of home, the enjoyment of wealth and learning, even the kindly recognition of his fellow citizens, were by him accounted as naught compared with duty. He lived to see justice triumphant, freedom universal, and to receive the tardy praises of his former opponents. The blessings of the poor, the friendless and the oppressed enriched him. In Boston he was born 29 November, 1811, and died 2 February, 1884. This tablet was erected in 1894, by order of the City Council of Boston."

The tributes of respect at the time of his death were such as were rarely, if ever before, paid to any private citizen. Flags in

Boston were at half mast, at the time of the funeral business was largely suspended, and the streets were thronged with people as his body was taken from the Hollis Street Church, where services were held, to lie in state in Faneuil Hall, where he won his first great oratorical triumph.

His illness had been so brief, his body not at all wasted, as I stood by its side with a few friends, in his chamber, in Common Street, before its removal to the church, he looked as one in a pleasant, restful sleep, majestic and strikingly beautiful even in death.

The church would hold but a small fraction of those eager to be admitted. The services, simple and impressive, were conducted by the Rev. Samuel Longfellow, of Cambridge, assisted by Rev. Samuel May, of Leicester, Mass. Among those present were the Governor of Massachusetts, deputations from both branches of the Legislature, the Mayor and Common Council, with many distinguished citizens, and representatives of the anti-slavery, temperance, woman suffrage, prison

and other philanthropic and reformatory organizations with the work of which Mr.
Phillips had been identified. The Robert
Shaw Veteran Association, colored, acted as
a bodyguard, accompanying the procession,
from the church, and at Faneuil Hall. Many
thousands filed past the coffin for a last look
at his face, and other thousands were awaiting
admission, as the time arrived for closing the
doors of the hall.

The remains of Mr. Phillips, which were
placed for a time in the family tomb in the
old Granary burying ground, Boston, were
subsequently interred in the same grave with
those of Mrs. Phillips, whose death occurred
in May, 1886, on a sunny hillside, commanding a wide and beautiful prospect,
in the Milton Cemetery, a few miles from
Boston.

Wendell Phillips lived the life of the philanthropist and agitator, with no vantage ground
of official position. There was no office,
however desirable, he might not have had, if
he would have consented to walk in the path-

way of political preferment. His was the
higher aim.

His eloquent memorial tribute to Mr. Garrison may also fitly be applied to himself. He
said :

"We lift a man to the pedestal of office and
imagine that that distinction will write his name
forever upon the records of his time. But the
only distinction which lasts is that which links
itself with some great idea, some effort of humanity
to lift itself in essential characteristics above its
former level—one of the great epochs, when humanity breaks a chain, frees itself from some
ignominious bondage, leaps up to the sunlight of
a grand deliverance."

It was to this level of true greatness which
Mr. Phillips himself, in a pre-eminent degree,
attained.

As Lowell so beautifully says of him :

" He stood upon the world's broad threshold; wide
    The din of battle and of slaughter rose;
He saw God stand upon the weaker side
    That sank in seeming loss before its foes;
Many there were who made great haste and sold
    Unto the common enemy their swords;

He scorned their gifts of fame, and power and
    gold,
  And, underneath their soft and flowery words,
Heard the cold serpent hiss; therefore he went
  And humbly joined him to the weaker part,
Fanatic named, and fool, yet well content
  So he could be the nearer to God's heart,
And feel its solemn pulses sending blood
    Through all the wide-spread veins of endless
    good."

CHAPTER IV.

My first anti-slavery lecturing campaign
included, beside the meetings already referred
to, an extended series in Western and in
Central New York. These were supple-
mented by others, during the latter part of
the winter and the spring of 1855, in Eastern
and Northern New York, in Columbia, Saratoga, Washington and Clinton Counties, and
later still, by meetings on Long Island, and
in Westchester and Dutchess Counties. I
had many experiences pleasant to recall in
memory of kindly welcomes in hospitable
homes, of valued new friendships formed, of
helpful co-operation in confessedly difficult,
but most needy fields for the labor of the
abolitionist. I had also not a little of the
other sort, much pro-slavery, ignorant, unreas-
oning, negro-hating prejudice to encounter,
unscrupulous misrepresentation by pro-slavery
politicians, and the cold shoulder from con-

servative, timid and time-serving ministers
and members of churches, then in guilty
complicity with slavery, and social ostracism
on the part of eminently "respectable" people,
who cared much more for " Mrs. Grundy"
than for the wrongs and suffering of the
outraged and defenseless slave. In Clinton
County my coming upon the anti-slavery
mission was announced in one of its journals,
with capital letters, under the heading "A
Stray Hottentot!"

In accordance with Wendell Phillips' suggestion to me, as a young speaker, to write
regularly, for the mental discipline, and, from
the anti-slavery field to write for the *National
Anti-Slavery Standard*, I followed his advice,
and began a correspondence.

Sidney Howard Gay was then editor of *The
Standard*, with Edmund Quincy as corresponding editor. Mr. Gay was of New
England birth and Harvard training, a gifted,
cultured writer, and a journalist of superior
ability. He had prepared himself for the
practice of law, and was ready for admission

to the bar, but becoming also deeply interested in the anti-slavery cause, was conscientiously constrained to turn from the legal profession, on account of the pro-slavery compromises of the Constitution of the United States, and what would be involved, and for a time was one of the American Anti-Slavery Society's lecturing agents. He brought to the *Anti-Slavery Standard* a high order of intelligence, and gave to it a literary excellence which more than maintained the reputation it had won, in this particular, under the previous editorship of Lydia Maria Child. It was during Mr. Gay's administration that Horace Greeley is said to have remarked of the fourth page of *The Standard*—its literary page—that it was "the best literary page in America."

My first letter to the *National Anti-Slavery Standard* was also my first experience in writing for the press. It gave in detail, with much too elaborate comments for correspondence, an account of my initial lecturing experience in Ontario, Alleghany and Cattaraugus Counties. Nor had I the slightest idea how much space it would all call for. It was, however, with great consideration on the part of the editor, printed entire, completely filling two of *The Standard's* very long columns. In due time it found its way to me in Western New York, where I was still lecturing. I recall vividly even now, more than forty years later, my sense of mortification and regret as I opened the paper and saw at a glance the manifestly disproportionate length of my letter—more than twice too long! My next was less than half its length, and much more appropriate to *The Standard's* space. After my second letter I received a message of friendly criticism and suggestion from Mr. Gay, which I valued highly, have treasured carefully, and from which I quote the following :

You will have observed that your letters have appeared in *The Standard.* I hope you have been long enough in harness to have got a thick skin on, and can bear criticism. Because I am moved to say—with your permission—that the last letter was the best, and better adapted to our correspondence columns than the first. The letters of an agent—if you will pardon me for making the suggestion—should be full of *facts;* of course the more they are of general interest the better, but facts rather than disquisitions, relations rather than reflections. It is the privilege of a letter-writer to be lively and discursive, critical and even censorious sometimes; while editors only are allowed to be solemn and dull. It is just the difference between the Rostrum and the Pulpit. Here you must labor to instruct, and stand on your dignity; there you are expected to amuse, at the same time you are instructive, and may throw dignity to the dogs.

I hope you will not think I take an unwarrantable liberty in saying this. A lecturing agent has great opportunity for good letters, but they are apt to think that they must talk in their letters as they do in their lectures, whereas, as it seems to me, the lectures are only the opportunity through which they may gather material for pleasant letters—sometimes for general reading, sometimes for the reading specially of the people to whom they have been lecturing.

I am, very truly,
Your friend,
S. H. Gay.

To one as young, and needing both experience and instruction, as was I, such a letter of frank and friendly counsel was most helpful and grateful.

Mr. Gay, in 1857, joined the editorial staff of the *New York Tribune*, and from 1862 to 1866 he was its managing editor. It was from him that, in 1865, I received a commission to represent *The Tribune*, as a member of the *Oceanus* excursion party on the occasion of the reraising of the flag at Sumter.

In 1867 Mr. Gay went to Chicago, where he was for several years managing editor of the *Chicago Tribune.* Returning again to New York early in the seventies, he became for a time managing editor of the *New York Evening Post.* Beside his very successful career in journalism, he made valuable contributions to historical and other literature, among which were " A Popular History of the United States," and a " Life of James Madison."

Edmund Quincy, who added largely, by his editorial contributions and as correspondent, to the influence and usefulness of *The Standard*, was, like Mr. Phillips, a graduate of Harvard University, of which his father,

Josiah Quincy, was a former president. He also was profoundly stirred by the murder of Lovejoy, and was moved to join the abolitionists at a time when such an accession to their ranks was indeed a great encouragement and strength. He was a man of fastidious tastes, loving a quiet life, educated as a lawyer, but living rather as a gentleman of leisure, not one who would be expected to join the ranks of the fanatics. He was a genial, efficient presiding officer, who added dignity, grace and a pleasant personnel to the sometimes tumultuous meetings of the abolitionists in Boston and New York.

It was in the autumn of 1855 that, by appointment, as a representative of the American Anti-Slavery Society, I attended, with Stephen S. Foster and others, the annual meetings of the Western Anti-Slavery Society, at Alliance, Ohio, and of the Michigan Anti-Slavery Society, at Battle Creek, Mich., and also an extended series of anti-slavery meetings in Ohio, Indiana and Michigan. It was my first experience of Western meetings and travel, then more than now quite in contrast, in unconventionality, with Eastern ways. West and East alike, however, felt the influence of the heavy hand of slavery, in both political and religious circles.

At the great meeting of the Western Anti-Slavery Society, at Alliance, Ohio, held in a large tent, and attended by fully five thousand people, I met very pleasantly Marius R. Robinson, editor of the *Anti-Slavery Bugle*, Charles S. S. and Josephine Griffing, Dr. Abram Brook, James Barnaby, Joel McMillain, Benjamin and J. Elizabeth Jones, Joseph Walton, Secretary of the Michigan Anti-Slavery Society, and others, of our Western coadjutors, whom I had not previously known personally. There were also present at this meeting from the East, beside Mr. Foster and myself, Mary Grew, of Philadelphia, and Henry C. Wright, of Boston. There were strong currents and counter-currents of feeling among the people, much sensitiveness to the criticisms, political and religious, of the abolitionists, but also much sympathy with the strongest anti-slavery appeals.

Beside the educational influence of the distinctively anti-slavery organizations, the anti-slavery public sentiment of Ohio, especially of the Western Reserve, had been greatly quickened and strengthened by the pronounced and very effective anti-slavery teaching, in and out of Congress, by Hon. Joshua R. Giddings, whose home was in Jefferson, Ashtabula County. As early as 1842 Mr. Giddings, on account of his opposition to slavery, was subjected to a vote of censure, at the instance of the incensed slaveholders of the House of Representatives, was denied a hearing by that body, resigned his seat, but was triumphantly returned by his Ohio constituents, and was kept in Congress, as the Representative of the Sixteenth Congressional District, for the full period of twenty years. His brave utterances and heroic example, from the vantage ground of the National House of Representatives, exerted a powerful anti-slavery influence throughout the country.

Differing in method, he was in spirit quite in unison with the most pronounced of the abolitionists.

It was one of the specially interesting incidents of this, my first visit to Ohio, that it was, in connection with my meetings in Ashtabula County, my privilege to be most cordially welcomed in the Giddings home. Mr. and Mrs. Giddings were absent, and my hostesses were the two daughters, Maria Giddings, the elder, a woman of great force of character, closely associated with the abolitionists, and Laura Giddings, the younger, then a very lovely young woman, with many of the characteristics of her honored father, by whom she was much beloved, and who subsequently became the wife of Hon. George W. Julian, to whom I shall again refer. Her friendship, commencing with this visit and continuing till her death, was one of the choicest of my life.

With Messrs. Foster and Philleo, sometimes attended by C. S. S. Griffing, as representing the Western Anti-Slavery Society, I attended many meetings, under varying conditions, in several counties in Ohio, in Northwestern Pennsylvania, in Northern Indiana, and in Michigan. In many localities were eager, sympathetic listeners, in others most outspoken, zealous, and sometimes violent opponents. In one Ohio neighborhood, at West Unity, I remember a meeting which I attended alone, as the only speaker, where I encountered several people who were formerly Virginians, and who were much excited that an abolitionist should appear for a hearing in their midst. The meeting was convened in a large school house, which served also on occasions as a public hall for meetings. There was a full attendance, with rumors of disturbance from without. A door of entrance opened directly opposite the speaker's platform. During the progress of the meeting it developed that a plan had been arranged by the outside disturbers to have one of their number, a former slaveholder, inside, near this door, which at a given signal, he would suddenly throw wide open, when I was to be pelted with eggs, thrown from without. It happened, however, that this inside sentinel, a man who had conceived a very strong prejudice against abolitionists, but had never before heard one speak, found himself much interested in what I had to say, and not disposed to interrupt me as had been planned. The outsiders, armed with eggs and receiving no promised signal, became weary of waiting and sent one of their own number to throw open the door. Quick as a flash, however, it was closed by the inside watcher, who knew what to expect, and just in time for it to receive the volley of eggs intended for myself! He then went outside and told the disturbers that he had mistaken the character of the meeting, and that they must keep quiet. They offered no further disturbance during the meeting, but agreed that I should receive their eggs at its close as I should leave for my lodgings. In this they were also thwarted by the one who they supposed would be their leader, and who, with others formed a bodyguard and conducted me, safe from disturbance, to the house where I was to be entertained.

It was while attending anti-slavery meetings which had been arranged for me in the counties of Northwestern Pennsylvania, adjacent to Ohio, that I was very kindly welcomed to a home for entertainment, the hostess of which, a sensible, intelligent woman, told me of her experience of a few years previous in having apparently died—an experience which would be of interest to members of the "Society for Psychical Research." That Society did not then exist, and I have no definite, exact notes of her statement, such as it would require, for its benefit. In substance it was to the effect that she had for a considerable period been a chronic invalid; that she subsequently had an acute illness, during which she suffered much, and finally, to all appearance, died. Her body became cold, the family gathered about the death-bed had, with much sorrow, accepted her death as a reality, and the physician, who had been in attendance, having done all in his power, had taken his departure. A friend in performing last offices for the body thought she detected warmth, the physician was hastily re-summoned and confirmed her suspicion, restoratives were applied, a little later, I do not remember just how long, my informant returned to full, conscious possession of her body. But, as she told me, she had been at no time personally unconscious. She knew what had transpired, of the grief of her family at her supposed death, but was conscious also of a new life, delightful and grateful quite beyond her power to describe. Her relief from the sense of bodily pain was great, as was her enjoyment of the new environment. Finally it seemed to be made known to her that she might, at her option, either return and take full possession of her body, with which she still had, through the brain, a slight connection, or she could sever altogether the cord which held her to it and go on in the new and very attractive life. Her love for, and sympathy with, her sorrowing and devoted family and friends turned the scale, and she decided to return and re-possess her body. She said it was at this moment, of mental decision, that the friend in attendance detected the returning warmth which culminated in full bodily rehabilitation. She was soon restored to a good degree of health, which she had since enjoyed. It was several years later that I saw her real death publicly announced.

The Western rural travel, in the rainy autumn or springtime, was at times, forty years ago, something formidable. It was before the era of bicycles and good road making, of which they have been the forerunner. I have still a vivid memory of some of the old "corduroy" roads, especially those of Northern Indiana, over which we traveled in fulfilling appointments for anti-slavery meetings, and of the necessity to cling vigilantly to the seat to keep from being quite thrown from the wagon into the apparently bottomless mud!

The Michigan Anti-Slavery Society's Annual Meeting for 1855, held in October, at Battle Creek, which it was also my privilege to attend and address, was rendered a notable, influential occasion by the presence and stirring addresses of William Lloyd Garrison, Charles C. Burleigh, Henry C. Wright, Stephen S. Foster and Marius R. Robinson, editor of the *Anti-Slavery Bugle.*

One of my prolonged journeys, in the winter of 1856, occupying several weeks, with Jacob Walton, Jr., Secretary of the Michigan Anti-Slavery Society, for a series of pioneer anti-slavery appointments in that State, extended from Pontiac, not far from Detroit, in the East, to Grand Rapids in the West, and inclusive of Lansing, the State capital, was accomplished by wagon, before a railroad had yet been constructed, through what was then a "new" portion of the State, with still very primitive conditions in the home life of many of the pioneer settlers. While out upon this "exploring expedition" we had at times intensely cold weather, and we were very forcibly reminded of the fate of Sir John Franklin's Expedition in the Arctic regions! In many of the places visited ours were the first anti-slavery meetings ever held there.

Some of them, at this distance of time, with slavery abolished, and the whole attitude of the public mind changed towards it, may now seem to have been inconsequential, but they were in reality quite otherwise. It was by the holding of very many such meetings, and the dissemination through them of anti-slavery literature, that here and there new converts were won, and that, finally, public sentiment was so educated and revolutionized as to make the abolition of slavery a possibility.

CHAPTER V.

THE Pennsylvania Anti-Slavery Society, outside of New England, was the strongest and most influential among the State auxiliaries of the American Anti-Slavery Society. I attended sundry meetings in Philadelphia, in the earlier period of my anti-slavery labor, and later occasional meetings in the Eastern counties. I shared, however, but to a limited extent in its general campaign work.

It was my privilege to attend and address the Pennsylvania Anti-Slavery Society's Twenty-third Annual Meeting, held in West Chester, in 1859. It was presided over by its venerable and beloved president, James Mott. Among the speakers were Lucretia Mott, Mary Grew, Robert Purvis, Rev. William H. Furness, Charles C. Burleigh, Rev. O. B. Frothingham, Rev. Samuel Longfellow, James Miller McKim, Edward M. Davis, Joseph A. Dugdale, Thomas Whitson, and others. The meeting was held during two days, in the Horticultural Hall, and the audiences during the several sessions were large, of thoughtful earnest people. A prominent topic under consideration in that meeting was the movement to make Pennsylvania a Free State by the enactment of a Personal Liberty Law, similar to one which had lately been placed upon the statute books of Vermont. This was a type of legislation then claiming much consideration in some of the more anti-slavery States of the North to protect fugitive slaves and practically to nullify the odious Fugitive Slave Law of 1850.

The most kind and friendly welcome extended to me at this meeting by James and Lucretia Mott, and by others of the Pennsylvania abolitionists, on the occasion of this my first visit to West Chester, forty years ago, is still a most pleasant memory.

Lucretia Mott, whose maiden name was Coffin, was born on Nantucket ; was educated in part, and subsequently became a teacher, at the Nine Partners Boarding School, in Dutch-

LUCRETIA MOTT.

ess County, N. Y., a school for both boys and girls, under the care of the Society of Friends. In this school James Mott, whose birthplace was Long Island, N. Y., was also a teacher. It was here that the acquaintance began which subsequently ripened into a marriage in which both husband and wife were greatly blessed. A business opening, to which James was invited, took them to Philadelphia, where, either in the city or its suburbs, during the more than half a century of their married life, they continued to reside. Their home, characterized by simplicity, with the atmosphere of refinement and culture, dominated by love, blessed largely not only the children born to it, but many friends to whom its generous, uplifting hospitality was so freely dispensed. Vivid among my own early anti-slavery memories is the first glimpse I had of it as a guest, with others, at the time of one of the great anti-slavery meetings in Philadelphia. In the spacious dining room, at one end of the long table sat Lucretia Mott as hostess, at the other James Mott as our host, with William Lloyd

Garrison, Wendell Phillips, Dr. William H. Furness, Mary Grew, Robert Purvis and others among the guests, and all made to feel quite at ease. Lovely and beloved as was Lucretia Mott in her public service, she was not less, but even more ideal in her home life. She was a delightful hostess, and had the gift of leading and keeping the conversation general for the interest and entertainment of all.

I recall also how, in a quiet way, toward the end of the dinner, during the period of the dessert, she had the earlier dishes, which had been removed and washed, returned to her, to be dried by her own hands, thus herself relieving the heavily taxed kitchen maids, meanwhile bearing her full share with her guests in the most engaging table talk! It was a memorable picture, a complete refutation of the criticism which used often to be made, and which still survives in certain quarters, to the effect that the woman who goes upon the public platform and shares in public service must needs be an inferior housekeeper and home maker.

Together James and Lucretia Mott welcomed William Lloyd Garrison in Philadelphia, on his return journey to Boston from Baltimore, after his imprisonment in the latter city. Later, in 1833, together they attended the National Anti-Slavery Convention at which was organized the American Anti-Slavery Society. Robert Purvis, who was also a member of that historic convention, not long before his death, in giving me some account of its proceedings and incidents, referred to Lucretia's helpful part in it with the greatest admiration. He said that as she sat, busy with her knitting, as was her wont on such occasions, when the various documents submitted for adoption were under consideration, she made sundry suggestions for amendment, the change of a phrase, or the substitution of a word here and there, all of which were readily and unanimously accepted and adopted. James Mott's name is among the signers of the Convention's Declaration, but Lucretia, being a woman, was not asked, or then expected to sign. Subsequently these two royal souls shared together many perils and sacrifices in their prolonged and devoted service in the anti-slavery reform. They also attended together the World's Anti-Slavery Convention in London, in 1840, in which Lucretia, and other regularly accredited women delegates from America, were not allowed to take seats.

Lucretia Mott was, in a very important sense, a pioneer in the movement to secure equal rights for women. As a teacher, she was made to feel early in life the inequality between the sexes in the matter of compensation for a kindred service. The opposition to the equal recognition of women in anti-slavery circles in this country, as well as in London, much impressed her with the need and importance of organized effort to secure equality of rights, the repeal or amendment of unequal laws, and full enfranchisement for women. She joined with Mrs. Stanton, Martha C. Wright (a younger sister of Lucretia Mott), and others, in holding a Woman's Rights Convention, at Seneca Falls, N. Y., as early as July 19 and 20, 1848. James Mott presided over this convention, which at that time was greeted with much ridicule. Lucretia lived to see many of the unequal and unjust laws affecting women amended, and a great change in the current of popular feeling concerning woman's full and equal enfranchisement. These beneficent changes were greatly promoted by her own judicious advocacy, and the powerful, exemplary influence of her own true and beautiful womanhood.

The Peace movement also enlisted very fully her sympathy, and to it she gave much helpful co-operation. She strongly deprecated war, and in her public ministry among Friends, and in Peace meetings and conventions, bore a faithful, effective testimony in favor of arbitration, and everywhere upheld the Christian teaching of " peace on earth and good will among men."

She was also deeply interested in the temperance reform, and gave to it, beside her personal example of abstinence from intoxicating beverages, much valuable public aid and encouragement.

Lucretia Mott, as a religious teacher in the Society of Friends, was without a peer in modern times. Liberal in thought, catholic in spirit, persuasive and truly eloquent in utterance, patient with prejudiced opposition, and sometimes marked discourtesy, she exerted a mighty transforming influence, so that in the later years of her ministry in the Society she was everywhere welcomed with tokens of respect and affection. Especially was she greatly beloved and reverenced by the younger Friends, with whom she always kept in closely sympathetic touch.

At the time of her visit to England in 1840 she encountered not a little prejudice on account of her well known liberal religious opinions. A curious instance of this is recorded in Haydon's Autobiography, a copy of which I was shown in a London library by an English friend, who knew and greatly esteemed her. B. R. Haydon, a well known artist of that period, who had been secured by some members of the convention to paint a picture of its opening, had sittings from various persons, more or less representative, for this purpose. Among these selected ones was Lucretia Mott. The artist, whose first impressions of her were evidently pleasant, intended to give her a conspicuous place in his historic sketch, but changed his mind for the reason given in the following diary note, which appears in his autobiography:

" 29th.—Lucretia Mott, the leader of the delegate women from America, sat. I found her out to have infidel notions, and resolved at once, narrow minded or not, not to give her the prominent place I first intended. I will reserve that for a beautiful believer in the Divinity of Christ."

In the large painting made by him, which I saw last year in the National Gallery, London, one figure is indicated, in an accompanying chart, as that of Lucretia Mott, but as given in a group in the distance, it is neither prominent nor recognizable. He subsequently painted a portrait of her for the Duchess of Sutherland.

At the close of the Pennsylvania Anti-Slavery Society's anniversary at West Chester in 1859 to which I have referred, it was my privilege to journey with Lucretia Mott by carriage, as guests of Joseph A. Dugdale, and to attend with her an appointed anti-slavery meeting at Longwood, Pa. The Longwood meeting of "Progressive Friends" was one outgrowth of the anti-slavery agitation, which as resisted by the more conservative Friends in Chester County, resulted in the disownment of several of the more radical and aggressive abolitionists of the body. Lucretia and myself were most cordially welcomed at this special meeting which had been appointed for us, and I then became acquainted also with a group of choice friends—the Coxes, Pennocks, Dugdales, Mendenhalls, Darlingtons, and others with whom I enjoyed very pleasant relations in subsequent years, among whom are still Samuel and Deborah Pennock and Lydia and Anna Cox of Kennett Square. It is an interesting fact that in 1874 the Kennett Monthly Meeting of Friends, unsolicited, extended an official invitation to Samuel Pennock and other of the surviving " disowned " abolitionists to be reinstated and again become members of the Meeting, an invitation which was accepted in the kindly spirit in which it was given.

From Longwood I accompanied Lucretia to Wilmington, Delaware, where we were guests of Thomas Garrett, chief among the representatives and managers of the " Underground Railroad."

Thomas Garrett, who was a member of the Society of Friends, was also a pronounced opponent of slavery, one of the strongest pillars and one of the most efficient working members of the American Anti-Slavery Society. A resident of a Border Slave State, a man of great tact, resource, and undaunted courage, moral and physical, he was truly a Moses to a multitude of fugitives from slavery, and a terror to their masters. At the time of the abolition of slavery he had preserved a record of twenty-five hundred and forty-five fugitives whom he had helped to escape from slavery, and he had assisted something over two hundred others, before he commenced the preservation of the remarkable record!

At the age of sixty he was deprived of all his property, through the machinery of the pro-slavery courts, on account of his befriending fugitive slaves, but such was the confidence and esteem which his heroic, upright character commanded, that he had the needed capital at once proffered by friends to continue his business—hardware—in which he was much prospered, was able to make good all his losses, and to enjoy a comfortable competence. He was a man of discriminating intelligence, of firmness as well as kindliness, and with little respect for, or patience with, shams of any kind, in religious, political or social life. I very much enjoyed this visit in his hospitable home.

From Wilmington I returned with Lucretia to Philadelphia, and attended with her the mid-week Friends' meeting at Fifteenth and Race streets, where were in attendance several hundred children, scholars of the Friends' School. It was a most attractive, beautiful picture of young life. On our way to the meeting Lucretia said to me that if I should feel that I had anything to say to the children she hoped I would be quite free to say it. I did feel on seeing them that I had a brief message for them, to which they listened with kindly attention. Lucretia followed, and told them of my anti-slavery labors, as a young man, etc. She in turn was followed by a rather conservative Friend, who had not then been fully converted to the anti-slavery gospel, whose communication seemed somewhat to discount both Lucretia and myself. To Lucretia this was no new experience, but to myself, at that time, it was somewhat as though a bucket of cold water had been poured over me!

It was a decade later and a little more, in January, 1871, that I was again in Wilmington with Lucretia Mott, this time to attend, by invitation, the funeral of our dear friend Thomas Garrett. He had in the intervening period of my anti-slavery labors been to me, indeed, as "a Father in Israel." The tributes paid to his memory by his fellow citizens, of all classes, white and colored, were something remarkable. For two hours before his body was taken from the house a continuous stream of humanity passed around the coffin to take a last look at the face of him whom they so much esteemed and honored. Then, borne upon the shoulders of stalwart colored men, who had asked the privilege, it was taken at the head of a procession through streets thronged with citizens, to the Friends' Meeting House, where funeral services were held, which only a small fraction of those desiring could attend, and thence to its final resting place in the adjacent burial plot. At this funeral service Lucretia Mott's presence and her words were, indeed, as a benediction.

Edward M. Davis, closely associated with James and Lucretia Mott, in family relationship and in the anti-slavery and other reform movements, was one of the most executive of the Pennsylvania abolitionists, whose acquaintance I formed early and whose continued friendship I prized highly. He was a forceful speaker, but also brought to the anti-slavery movement the executive efficiency of a successful man of business. As a business man he was the soul of honor, and justly esteemed for his uprightness of character. He was often introduced as " Lucretia Mott's son-in-law," a distinction which he was wont humorously to refer to, and much enjoyed. He was a man of great kindness of heart and tenderest sympathy.

After the abolition of slavery, he extended, in a brotherly spirit, his helpful co-operation in my special work in the temperance reform, and also with our New York Committee for the Prevention of State Regulation of Vice, though he shrank from the discussion of that subject. In a letter from Philadelphia, accompanying a contribution in aid of the work of that Committee, and in response to an invitation to one of our earlier meetings at the "Isaac T. Hopper Home" in New York, he wrote:

"I cannot be present, and if I could I fear I should not be, for I have not risen to the position to be able to *discuss* this terrible question in what we call a mixed assembly when we mean of both sexes, but I honor all those who can, and especially those who do what is called and is really the work

in this important matter. So I send a mite en-
closed, just to satisfy my conscience, for I know it
is my duty to do something in some direction, so
like all cowards or drones I accept the easiest
way."

In a letter when he was nearing the close
of his life, and we were meeting less frequently
than at an earlier period, referring to our long
continued relation of friendship he wrote :

"Although I may seldom see you or your wife,
if you think of me as often as I do of you, we keep
up a very friendly and frequent correspondence."

And at the close of another letter of this
period he said : "If I could only *feel* old, I
would say, with the blessings of an old man."

Mary Grew, whom it was also my privilege
early to know as a personal friend, was an
exceptionally gifted speaker and writer, whose
labors, with both voice and pen, were most
influential and helpful in behalf of the slave,
both within and beyond the domain of the
Pennsylvania Anti-Slavery Society. Less
familiarly, I knew also her honored father,

Rev. Henry Grew. Both were fellow voyagers with James and Lucretia Mott to the World's Anti-Slavery Convention in London in 1840. Of the Philadelphia Female Anti-Slavery Society, organized the year after the American Anti-Slavery Society, of which Lucretia Mott was for many years the president, Mary Grew was secretary during a kindred period and until its final dissolution upon the abolition of slavery. Her annual reports were models of their kind, and have a permanent value for students as contributions to anti-slavery history. She rendered valuable anti-slavery service as joint editor, with James Miller McKim, of the *Pennsylvania Freeman*. I also received from her, from time to time, assistance most grateful during my own editorship of the *National Anti-Slavery Standard* the last years of its publication. As a speaker she was persuasive, logical and convincing, morally courageous, equal to any emergency, but less aggressive and denunciatory than some of her compeers on the anti-slavery platform.

She was deeply interested in, and aided efficiently, the efforts to secure enlarged opportunities for women, industrial, civil and political. She also gave to us most grateful and helpful sympathy and co-operation in our work for the repression of vice and the promotion of purity, alike for both sexes.

She was much interested in liberal religious thought, and a gifted interpreter of spiritual truth, occupying occasionally, in the later years of her life, pulpits to which she was invited. In this direction she recognized her indebtedness to Lucretia Mott. In a letter to the latter, after the death of James Mott, she wrote:

"If I were to try, I could never tell you, dear friend and teacher, how much you have done for me. The breaking of some spiritual fetters, the parting of some clouds which opened deeper vistas into heaven, I owe to you.

Some day, perhaps, in this world or another, sitting at your feet, I can tell you more of this. Now, sorrowing in your sorrow, I can do little more than pray that you may be blessed and comforted, even as you have blessed and comforted others."

In a letter of deep and tender sympathy to my wife and myself when we were suffering from a severe bereavement, accompanying a volume, which she hoped might be helpful to us, in that period of sore need, as it had been to her, she made this comment, indicating also her own thought of God:

"The worst feature of it is that worst feature of our prevailing theology, which represents our God and Father in a character unworthy of those dear names. When I am pained and oppressed with the thought of the blindness and ignorance of so large a part of the leaders of the church, and wonder at their miserable conceptions of the character of God, which lead them to regard theological dogmas as far more important than a Christ-like spirit and life, I console myself with a view of the immense progress which mankind has made, in this respect, within a few centuries. The heretics of a hundred years ago are the orthodox of to-day. Though theological shells are called, still, by their old names, their kernels are so changed, by the ripening process of the years, that their 'sponsors in baptism,' who gave them those names, would not know them now. My double metaphor is perfectly shocking; I guess it wrote itself; at any rate I decline being sponsor for it!"

In a letter to my wife, referring to our relation of personal friendship, greatly prized by my wife as myself, she wrote:

"Your and Mr. Powell's photographs lie on my table, making me wish that they could speak to me. Mr. Powell's looks as if it would, but it does not. How good they both are! I believe I sent you my thanks for them, last summer, when writing to Mr. Powell, but I repeat them now. It is rather late to answer the kind and welcome letter which contained them, as I have seen you since; but it is not too late to tell you that your letters are always welcome to me, and that I should highly value the privilege of frequent intercourse with you face to face. I am now looking forward to the pleasure of seeing you both here, at our Annual Meeting. Do not fail to come, we *need* you both; and it does us all good, I think, to meet on these occasions."

In another she wrote:

"It would have given me much pleasure to see you and Mrs. Powell, on my return from Providence. I like to remember my visit to your home."

Such friendships were, indeed, a rich compensation for the obloquy and ostracism for abolitionists which was linked with the anti-slavery conflict.

James Miller McKim, whom I knew less intimately, was educated for the ministry, and was for a brief period a Presbyterian minister. He attended the National Anti-Slavery Convention of 1833 in Philadelphia, and was one of the organizers of the American Anti-Slavery Society, subsequently becoming one of its Lecturing Agents. Later, as Corresponding Secretary and General Manager of the Pennsylvania Anti-Slavery Society, as editor of the *Pennsylvania Freeman* and Philadelphia correspondent of the *National Anti-Slavery Standard*, as agent of the Underground Railroad, and subsequently as an organizer of, and co-worker with, societies for the education of the Freedmen, he filled a sphere of exceptional usefulness.

Robert Purvis was another of the anti-slavery pioneers by whom I was very kindly welcomed to that field of service. Born in Charleston, S. C., his father a native of Northumberland, England, and his mother of Moorish descent, free-born, he was educated in the North, completing his education at

Amherst College, and subsequently residing in Philadelphia or its vicinity. He had rare oratorical gifts, marked dignity and grace of manner, and was always a welcome speaker in anti-slavery meetings and conventions. He was a member of the National Anti-Slavery Convention in Philadelphia, in 1833, and a signer of its Declaration, but still earlier had been a co-worker with Benjamin Lundy, against slavery. He chose to identify himself with the victim and enslaved race, though when he thus referred to himself his hearers would look at him with incredulity, so slight was the connecting link. Blessed with a pecuniary competence he was a generous helper in money, as well as in personal service, both of the Pennsylvania, and the American Anti-Slavery Society. He was public spirited, and highly esteemed by many of his fellow citizens, of the better class, not immediately identified with the anti-slavery movement. He was an earnest believer in equal rights for women, and a frequent and welcome speaker on the woman suffrage platform.

He was a genial host. In connection with one of my earliest visits to Philadelphia, many years ago, I was most kindly welcomed by him, and by his family, in their hospitable rural home of that period, at Byberry; a refuge and shelter also for many a fugitive from slavery, en route to Canada.

It was following this early visit to Byberry, that, accompanied by Mr. Purvis, I made my first visit also to Bristol, Pa., in the home of Cyrus and Ruth Peirce. They and their sons and daughters, intimate friends of and co-workers with Lucretia Mott, Robert Purvis and Mary Grew, were among the stalwart abolitionists of the time. It was an ideal Quaker home dedicated to high thought, and upright, exemplary living, to which were also welcomed from time to time William Lloyd Garrison, Wendell Phillips, Lucy Stone, Charles C. Burleigh, and other well known representatives of the anti-slavery and kindred reform movements. Associated with this home for a considerable period, under the care and direction of the daughters, Ruth Anna, (now Mrs. Ruth Anna Peirce DeCou,) Sarah and Fanny, was a very successful private school, of an exceptionally interesting character. Its fortunate students had not only first class intellectual advantages, but added thereto also a superior moral training. Despite the prevalent color prejudice, and threatened loss of patronage, colored students were received, sharing equally the opportunities afforded by the school. It was a delight to witness the well merited happiness of the venerable and venerated parents in their large family, of both sons and daughters.

Sarah H. Peirce, whose later years, with her sisters, were passed in Philadelphia, filled a place of much usefulness in the Society of Friends, of which she was a representative member,—as were her parents formerly,—as a helper in the cause of education for the colored people, for whose emancipation she had labored ; for the promotion of peace and arbitration ; temperance ; civilization for the

Indian, and the enfranchisement of women. She was a member of the General Council of the American Purity Alliance, and did much in quiet ways, especially in the judicious use of literature, to promote the purity movement. With physical disability which limited her later activity, her patient perseverance in making the uttermost of her opportunities to render helpful, generous service for others, especially the poor and lowly, was a rarely beautiful object lesson. Her messages to us when she could herself no longer hold and guide the pen, but expressed through the hand of another, were affectionate, inspiring and replete with spiritual strength.

Rev. William H. Furness, who was from an early period a prominent figure in anti-slavery circles, I knew less familiarly, but esteemed most highly. His presence in our anti-slavery meetings in Philadelphia, New York and elsewhere, was as a benediction. Of New England birth, the school companion in the Boston Latin School, the college-mate at Harvard and intimate life-long friend of

Ralph Waldo Emerson, he brought to the anti-slavery movement, as he took to his church in Philadelphia, intellectual culture of the finest quality, unflinching moral heroism, and an attractive personality, characterized by simplicity, sincerity, much kindliness and grace of manner. Between himself and Lucretia Mott was a very strong bond of personal friendship.

His high appreciation of her exalted character was many times expressed. A noteworthy instance was in a sermon preached after one of the very exciting fugitive slave trials in Philadelphia, the Dangerfield case, in which Lucretia sat by the side of the negro fugitive throughout the prolonged trial, wherein he said:

"I looked the other day into that low, dark and crowded room, in which one of the most wicked laws that man ever enacted was in process of execution, and there I beheld the living presence of that Spirit of Christ, out of which shall again grow the beautiful Body of Christ, the true church.

"The close and heated atmosphere of the place well became the devilish work that was going on.

The question was, whether, for no crime, but for the color of the skin which God gave him, a fellow-man should be robbed of his dear liberty and degraded to a chattel and a brute.

" There sat the man in his old hat and red flannel shirt and ragged coat, just as he was seized by the horrible despotism. There he sat, while questions were discussed involving things dearer to him than life. On one side of him stood the minister of the cruel law. On the other—the place was luminous to my soul with a celestial light—for there stood a devoted Christian woman, blind to all outward distinctions and defacements, deaf to the idle babble of the world's tongues, cheering her poor hunted brother with the sisterly sympathy of her silent presence.

" And as I looked upon her, I felt that Christ was there; that no visible halo of sanctity was needed to distinguish that simple act of humanity, done under such circumstances, as an act pre-eminently Christian, profoundly sacred, ineffably religious."

Dr. Furness presented to Swarthmore College a beautiful portrait of Lucretia, painted by his son, William Henry Furness, which now adorns the Assembly Hall of the College, of the founding of which she and James Mott were among the early promoters. In connection with the presentation of this portrait he says : " I used to be present when Lucretia had her sittings, and we had pleasant talks together. The book that she is represented as having open in her lap is a volume of Blanco White's Life and Letters, from which she read favorite passages aloud."

He lived to the advanced age of 92, and passed on to the larger life January 30, 1896. In a letter from a Philadelphia friend, Mrs. Charlotte S. Lewis, which I received the day following the largely attended funeral, she writes :

" We looked for the last time on the genial face of our dear old Dr. Furness to-day. An unusually beautiful life with a most fitting close—a falling to sleep in the arms of his loved Horace after a sweet smile of recognition. His character will live among us as a forcible lesson."

CHAPTER VI.

THE major portion of my service in the anti-slavery lecture field, and in meetings and conventions in behalf of the American Anti-Slavery Society, during the latter part of the fifties and early in the sixties, covering nearly a decade, was within the limits of the State of New York, with occasional visits in Pennsylvania, and in New England. I became quite familiar with nearly every part of the Empire State.

On Long Island I early had the co-operation, most kind and helpful, of Joseph and Mary W. Post and their family. In their very hospitable home at Westbury I was welcomed from time to time with a cordiality and freedom, which, in that period of general social ostracism for abolitionists, made it seem, indeed, like an oasis in the desert. They were exemplary, faithful members of the Society of Friends, and were also the warm personal friends of James and Lucretia Mott. Not only was I received in their home for entertainment, but they also opened their house for my meetings, at a time when the Friends' Meeting House, strange as it may now seem, was closed against them. Boards were brought in by Joseph and laid from chair to chair, and thus were the sittings increased to meet the needs of the occasion. A few white, and more colored people, some of them former slaves, constituted the audiences. They journeyed with me in their capacious carriage to Jericho, Jerusalem, and other adjacent towns, chiefly Friends' neighborhoods, for other meetings. On one occasion, now more than forty years ago, we drove to Jericho, where formerly lived Elias Hicks. We attended the mid-week Friends' meeting. At its close Joseph made a request for the use of the Meeting House for an anti-slavery meeting that evening. The attendance was not large; all present were individually willing, but collectively they were not free to give consent, because of some previous action of the Monthly Meeting against the opening of the meeting houses for anti-slavery meetings. It was therefore arranged that we should hold our meeting in a school-house, a mile or two distant. Every Friend in attendance at the meeting in the morning, though the evening proved dark and stormy, was present at our school-house meeting, among the number being a daughter of Elias Hicks, who expressed much interest.

We next visited Jerusalem, where then resided Arden Seaman, a well known, liberal minister among Friends. At Jerusalem, as at Jericho, there was the adverse Monthly Meeting rule against using the Friends' Meeting House for anti-slavery meetings, but Friend Seaman, who was of a rather heroic mould, decided that, Andrew Jackson like, he would "take the responsibility," and open the meeting house for our meeting. A few Friends and others came and we had a very good meeting.

Quiet and undemonstrative, Joseph and

Mary Post had much firmness blended with gentleness of character, and a faith which was undaunted, however formidable and immovable the opposition might appear to be.

Their active, helpful interest was not confined to the anti-slavery reform; they were ready to extend sympathy and aid to all humane, benevolent efforts. They were *real* Friends, and though in the earlier period of their lives they were often made to feel that they were in the minority, in their later years they were better understood, and by all held in much esteem. They were to me as a father and mother throughout my anti-slavery labors. They also extended to us grateful sympathy and most helpful co-operation in our later work for the promotion of purity, and an equal standard of morals for men and women. In a letter, accompanying a gener-ous contribution, at a time when a measure had been introduced in the New York Legislature to provide for State regulation of vice, not very long before her transition to the larger life, Mary wrote:

"I keep hoping for better times, but really it seems as though there never was a time when it was more needful to be on the alert to prevent evil legislation than the present. I have, with all the discouragements, felt that the world was growing better, and I see cause for hope, when from the pulpits we hear the severe arraignment by popular ministers of the evils prevailing.

"I hope *you workers* will keep up courage and work on, and, perhaps as in the past, your labors may prevent the legalizing of social vice. It would be dreadful. I thought our State stood on higher ground.

"I think *The Philanthropist* is doing a good work, perhaps more than previously, and among Friends too. Some who could not tolerate it or its editors seem quite friendly disposed. We shall miss —— ——'s influence; he was more interested in the movement than any other of our Friends.

"I cannot but hope you will succeed in getting a bill for a Reformatory for women. It seems to me every one must see the imperative need.

"I wish I could aid in all these labors, but my day is over—and indeed I never was of any help as a public advocate. I could *wish* it well, and hand the cup of cold water to the faithful."

What Joseph and Mary Post and family were to me in my early and later anti-slavery labors on Long Island, that were Joseph and Margaret Carpenter and family in Westchester

County. Joseph Carpenter was the "Friend Joseph" mentioned with so much appreciation by Lydia Maria Child in her *Romance of the Republic.* She was for a time, during the period of her editorship of the *National Anti-Slavery Standard*, an inmate of their very pleasant country home at Mamaroneck. She was for many years, and until her death, the intimate friend of the daughter, Esther Carpenter Pierce, who still survives in a serene, beautiful old age, at Pleasantville. It was the grand daughter, who bore the honored name of Lydia Maria Child Pierce, a young woman of much promise, who was of the first graduating class of Swarthmore College. Joseph Carpenter's Mamaroneck home was also one of the important stations on the " Underground Railway" and sheltered and helped on his or her way to freedom in Canada many an escaping fugitive from slavery.

My Westchester anti-slavery meetings, which were arranged for by Joseph Carpenter, and to which he accompanied me in Mamaroneck, New Rochelle, Port Chester, and at other points, were attended by limited audiences of white people, and by more colored people resident in the different localities. There was much prejudice against colored people in this region, so much, that at that time in New Rochelle colored people were denied burial in any of its cemeteries or burial places. To meet this difficulty Joseph Carpenter set apart a portion of one of the fields of his Mamaroneck farm as a burial plot for the colored people. By his direction his own body was interred therein. I visited him a short time previous to his death, when he acquainted me with this arrangement for the disposition of his body, as a last testimony against the then prevailing—and, alas, still prevalent—unchristian color prejudice. In accordance with his wish I also attended his funeral, and to those assembled bore my testimony to his memory and great personal worth. It was an occasion long to be remembered. His body, clothed in his wonted plain Friendly costume, was placed for burial, as he had also directed, in a plain, unstained pine coffin. At the conclusion of the services the coffin was carried out upon the lawn, in the shade of the trees he loved so well, and then those in attendance, colored and white, gathered about it to take a last look at the face of him whom they loved and reverenced. Then it was borne by colored men, who had requested the privilege, to its final resting place, among those of the proscribed colored people whom he had befriended.

At a later period the body of Margaret Carpenter, the wife, a woman of sterling worth, sharing fully the deep feeling of her husband concerning the great injustice from which the colored people, both bond and free, were sufferers, was also interred in this unique, and now historic, burial plot.

Joseph Carpenter suffered keenly, as a Friend, at the time of the disownment of Isaac T. Hopper, Charles Marriott, and James S. Gibbons, by the New York Yearly Meeting, on account of their connection with the Executive Committee of the American Anti-

Slavery Society, and the strictures upon pro-slavery Friends by its organ, the *National Anti-Slavery Standard.* He was so much pained by this proscriptive action, which he believed to be most uncalled for and unjust, that he never afterward felt at liberty to attend a Yearly Meeting in New York.

Gentle and lovable in spirit, he had a large circle of warmly attached personal friends, and had many requests for his photograph.

He had one photograph taken with a little colored boy, the child of a colored woman whom they had befriended, standing by him, and these he would give to friends from whom he had such requests, feeling that he was at the same time conveying silently the lesson he so much desired to teach concerning the cruel and unjust color prejudice.

Moses Pierce the son-in-law of Joseph and Margaret Carpenter, and Esther Carpenter Pierce, the daughter, and their family, of Pleasantville, sympathized warmly with the beloved father and mother in their interest in the anti-slavery, peace, temperance and other humane, reformatory movements. Their very hospitable home was also another of my own anti-slavery homes, wherein I have had a warm welcome and much kindness.

Moses Pierce was an active Friend, and at a New York Yearly Meeting a few years ago, not long before his death, he introduced a proposition, which it was my own privilege to second, to the effect that, slavery having been abolished, an appropriate minute be made acknowledging the error of the Yearly Meeting, at the time when pro-slavery prejudice was rife against the abolitionists, in disowning Isaac T. Hopper, Charles Marriott and James S. Gibbons. It was just as the meeting was about to adjourn, and the way did not appear to be open for the proposed action at that time. It would still be a creditable thing for the Yearly Meeting to do. As the record now stands the verdict of history is against it.

Esther Carpenter Pierce, upon whom largely the mantle of her beloved father descended, has, for a quarter of a century, since the

JOSEPH CARPENTER.

anti-slavery conflict culminated, been, as she still is, one of our most valued and sympathetic helpers in our mission for the promotion of purity.

It was early in the sixties that by invitation of Hon. John Jay I visited the Jay Homestead, in Westchester County. I was attending, in behalf of the American Anti-Slavery Society, a series of meetings, accompanied and assisted by my wife, Anna Rice Powell, and my sister, Elizabeth M. Powell (now Elizabeth Powell Bond, Dean of Swarthmore College), in Bedford, Mt. Kisco, and at other points in Westchester County and Eastern New York. Bedford is not far from the Jay Homestead, the former home also of Hon. William Jay. Mr. Jay was unable to attend the meeting, but sent a very kind message, and his carriage to take us to his historic home. We were shown many interesting mementoes of the honored father, Judge William Jay, and of the distinguished grandfather, Chief Justice John Jay, the first Chief Justice of the United States, with portions of the accumulated libraries of each. I have before me, as I write, a very interesting volume, " Miscellaneous Writings on Slavery," by William Jay, presented to me on the occasion of this visit, by John Jay. It is stated therein that the first society ever formed, it is believed, for the abolition of slavery, was organized in the city of New York, January, 1785, under the presidency of John Jay, the first Chief Justice. The principles of this pioneer society are indicated in the following declaration of its distinguished president:

"I wish to see all unjust and unnecessary discriminations everywhere abolished, and that the time may soon come, when all our inhabitants, of every COLOR and denomination, shall be free and EQUAL PARTAKERS OF OUR POLITICAL LIBERTY."

John Jay, who, subsequent to our visit, was appointed United States Minister to Austria, and who was for a prolonged period President of the Union League Club, was a high-minded, public spirited citizen, influential in public affairs, a man of much kindness of heart, a most genial host, and a worthy descendant of his honored progenitors.

During the decade following 1855 I attended and addressed, in behalf of the American Anti-Slavery Society, many meetings and conventions in the State of New York. In some of the meetings, at times, I was the only speaker, but generally, during these years, I was associated with others. My most intimate and constant associate for this period was Susan B. Anthony. Together we held meetings in many of the localities which I had previously visited during the first year or two of my anti-slavery service. In 1856 Miss Anthony was appointed a General Manager for an anti-slavery campaign in the State of New York, and an extended series of meetings was arranged for, to which Charles Lenox Remond and his sister, Sarah P. Remond, of Massachusetts, were assigned by the Executive Committee as speakers, in addition to Miss Anthony and myself.

Miss Anthony's previous limited public service had been mainly in connection with educational and temperance work, and, in an initial way, for the enfranchisement of women. She was deeply moved by the wrongs of the slave, and the cruel injustice of slavery, and dedicated herself most earnestly and unselfishly to the anti-slavery movement, quickened thereto especially by Stephen and Abby Kelley Foster, whose stirring meetings she had attended in Rochester and elsewhere. With much executive force she attended to the many and wearisome details and drudgery involved in such campaigning for an unpopular cause. In her previous public addresses she had been confined mainly to the use of manuscript; in these earlier anti-slavery meetings, which we attended together, she gained her first experience in extempore speaking, and not without a heroic struggle.

Of the prevalent cruel prejudice against color we had striking illustrations in connection with our meetings which were attended and addressed by Mr. and Miss Remond. Educated, refined and sensitive, they were continually and painfully reminded of the heartless and vulgar color prejudice. Hotels and boarding houses which would receive Miss Anthony and myself, rudely denied admission to them, and solely on the ground of color. On one occasion I recall being a guest, with the Remonds, in the home of anti-slavery friends in Washington County, N. Y. A neighbor called while we were there and gave a distressing account of a neglected family in the vicinity, sufferers from small-pox. On account of the dread disease, and the fear of contagion, others shrank from going to them to minister to their needs. Mr. Remond, at the conclusion of the painful narrative, after an expression of sympathy for the suffering, quietly, and with much significance remarked : " To colored people it is the same as having the small-pox all the time."

We were all subjected, more particularly during the winter months, to many discomforts, much exposure and not a little fatigue, especially in our journeying away from the larger cities and towns. I remember one ride of twenty-five miles in Northern New York, in mid-winter, in a stage sleigh, with closely buttoned curtains, no ventilation, and the mercury at thirty-two degrees below zero. There were several men among the passengers, who were very offensive in their use of tobacco. The driver, after an admonition that I might perish from the cold, finally allowed me to share his seat, and wraps, on the outside. Though the cold was intense, I escaped from the tobacco poisoning, was not actually frozen, and was able to meet my anti-slavery appointment in the evening.

Our real headquarters for these successive New York State anti-slavery campaigns, for the several years, if we may be said to have had any, were in Albany. Residing there were Lydia Mott, and her sister, Jane Mott, also Phebe H. Jones and Margaret, her daughter, closely in touch with the American Anti-Slavery Society. For a time also there was an Anti-Slavery Depository established in Albany, under the care of our dear friend, Lydia Mott. Albany, as the State capital, was also auspicious for our legislative work, especially during the " Personal Liberty " era, when we sought State protection for fugitives from slavery after the enactment of the infamous Fugitive Slave Law. Annual State Anti-Slavery Conventions were held in Albany for several successive years, with addresses at different times by representative speakers, among whom were Mr. Garrison, Wendell Phillips, Rev. Samuel J. May, Parker Pillsbury, the Fosters, Elizabeth Cady Stanton, Charles Lenox Remond, Rev. Beriah Green, Rev. A. D. Mayo, and others. These we regarded as auspicious occasions for reaching and interesting the legislators of the State, some of whom were generally in attendance, and through them the general public.

The anti-slavery centre of Western New York was the city of Rochester. Residing there, beside relatives and personal friends of mine, to whom I have already referred, were a group of earnest, faithful abolitionists, including Isaac and Amy Post, (brother of Joseph Post, of Long Island,) Frederick Douglass, William R. and Mary Hallowell,

Edmund and Sarah Willis, Benjamin and Sarah Fish, Giles B. Stebbins and Catharine A. F. Stebbins, Daniel and Lucy Anthony, (the father and mother of Susan B. Anthony,) Elias and Rhoda De Garmo, and others, all deeply interested in, and valuable helpers of, the anti-slavery, and other reforms.

It was during the autumn of 1858, when I was not quite equal in health to continuous anti-slavery campaigning, that, at the invitation of Susan B. Anthony, I passed the months of September and October in Rochester, and gave, in the Unitarian Church, a series of eight discourses upon liberal Christianity, in its various practical aspects. The details were efficiently arranged by Miss Anthony.

It was during the winter of 1860-61, after the election of Lincoln, and before his inauguration as President of the United States, that our anti-slavery conventions in the larger cities, Buffalo, Rochester, Auburn, Syracuse, Utica and Albany, were much disturbed by mobs. I have previously referred to our experience in Syracuse. The convention at Buffalo I was unable to attend, but assisted in the others. This unexpected and rather surprising revival of mob violence against the abolitionists was not confined to our conventions in New York, but developed also in Boston, against Wendell Phillips, who was speaking in Music Hall, and in other localities wherein abolitionists were announced to speak. It seemed in our New York experience as though the mobs in the several cities might have a common source of inspiration and direction. In Auburn we were driven from our hall by the suffocating fumes of red pepper thrown by the miscreants upon a hot stove. I happened to be upon the platform making an address at the time and could not get relief as soon as others who rushed quickly to open windows and doors. Suddenly it seemed as though a thousand needle points were penetrating my throat, which was for a time seriously affected, and with threatened loss of voice. At Utica we were not allowed by the mob to enter the hall, which had been engaged for our convention; and, as at Syracuse, we met in private parlors, by the kind invitation of Mr. and Mrs. J. C. De Long. A subsequent investigation, by one of our Utica friends, disclosed the fact that the evening prior to our convention in that city a group of men met in a lawyer's office and prepared resolutions, which were adopted by the mob the following day, and telegraphed over the country, by the Associated Press, declaring in substance that the people of Utica repudiated the abolitionists *and Lincoln*, and that the central figure of that group was none other than Horatio Seymour, the well known democratic leader, whose home was in Utica. It was further ascertained that these mobocratic demonstrations against abolitionists in Northern cities at this time were part of a scheme of a political organization, known as the "Knights of the Golden Circle," with headquarters in the South, to create a popular revolt against Lincoln, and to prevent his inauguration as President. President Lincoln was obliged, it will be remembered, to make his way incognito through Baltimore as he journeyed to Washington. It was also a significant fact that the name of Horatio Seymour appeared at this very time upon the subscription list of the *National Anti-Slavery Standard*, indicating his appreciation of the political influence of the movement, though quite independent of all partisan politics, which it represented.

These last mobs, with which we were confronted, proved to be the forerunner of the slaveholders' rebellion, which soon after developed, and with the end of which, after a great expenditure of blood and treasure, came the end, as a legalized institution, of slavery itself.

CHAPTER VII.

I HAD the pleasure of knowing John G. Whittier, the poet of the anti-slavery reform, and of meeting him from time to time during the later years of his life. At the time of his last visit to New York he called at the office of the *National Anti-Slavery Standard*, of which I was then editor, to see me, but, much to my regret, I was out and missed his call. He was then in feeble health, and left a message for me saying: "I would very much like to see thee, but I cannot climb these three flights of stairs again." During his sojourn with friends in Brooklyn, my wife and myself, by appointment, called later upon him. In general, and in large companies especially, he was shy and retiring. On this occasion we were alone with him, and, seated upon a sofa between us, it gave us the coveted opportunity to tell him, face to face, how grateful we were for the help some of

JOHN G. WHITTIER.

his consoling words had given us in a time of sore bereavement through which we had been passing. This seemed to unlock the storehouse of memory with him, and as we sat together in the evening quiet he told us somewhat of his own experiences in life, its sorrows and joys, out of which some of the poems, which have given so much comfort to many, were born. I wish it were possible to share this conversation with others. It was, as will be readily inferred, an occasion of deep interest to us, and very precious in memory.

On another occasion we met him under very different circumstances in Boston. It was at the time of the visit to the United States of Dom Pedro, Emperor of Brazil. The Emperor declined most proffered receptions and social functions, but he said to a friend, Mrs. Agassiz, that there was one whom he would be very glad to meet—the Quaker poet, John G. Whittier. The Emperor had become much interested in Whittier through his poetry, some of which he had translated.

The problem was how to induce Whittier to come to Boston, and to arrange for the meeting. He occasionally visited Rev. and Mrs. John T. Sargent, anti-slavery friends, and attended in their parlors the unique meetings of the Chestnut Street Radical Club, of which they were host and hostess. Mrs. Sargent had a genius for bringing people together, and it was arranged that she would give a reception in honor of the Emperor, to which Whittier, with Emerson, Longfellow, Holmes, Wendell Phillips, Lucy Larcom, and others of Boston's distinguished literati, were invited. We chanced to be in Boston, and, as friends of the Sargents, were privileged to be present. When the Emperor arrived he was met by the hostess and escorted by her to the parlors, which were on the second floor, and was introduced to one and another of the distinguished company in waiting, but with little apparent interest in any, until they came to Whittier, for whom he asked and whom he greeted with much enthusiasm, folding him in his arms. He then drew him to a seat and engaged most earnestly in conversation with him till his departure, giving relatively little heed to the presence of the other distinguished men and women who were there also to welcome him. When he must needs leave he asked Whittier to accompany him, and arm in arm they made their way from the parlors down the stairs, parting at the door. As the carriage bore him away the Emperor raised his hat and gave a parting salute to the house.

With his shy and shrinking tendency the ordeal was a trying one for Whittier, but all those present knew and loved him, and much appreciated the very marked attention which the Emperor had shown him.

Among the essayists who from time to time read papers at the meetings of the Chestnut Street Club were Ralph Waldo Emerson, John Weiss, David A. Wasson, Dr. Bartol, Samuel Longfellow, Oliver Wendell Holmes, Julia Ward Howe, Rev. W. H. Channing, Mary Grew, T. W. Higginson, Rev. O. B. Frothingham and others. The topics and discussions were sometimes very abstract, metaphysical and philosophical. At the conclusion of one of these meetings with, I think, John Weiss as essayist, much of the talk which followed having been peculiarly abstract and in the metaphysical clouds, Whittier, who sat near my wife and myself, as a quiet listener, commented to us upon the speculative character of the discussion, saying, with a significant twinkle in his eye: "I settled those things for myself long ago." Mrs. Claflin, in her "Personal Recollections," writes of him as once saying to her: "As I was walking across the floor at the Radical Club a woman stopped me in the middle of the parlor among all the folks and said, 'I've long wished to see you, Mr. Whittier, to ask you what you thought of the subjective and objective.' Why, I thought the woman was crazy, and I said 'I don't know anything about either of 'em.'"

At one of the meetings of the Club, when Mary Grew, of Philadelphia, was to read a paper upon "Essential Christianity," Whittier, who was closely associated with her in anti-slavery work during the period of his editorship of the *Pennsylvania Freeman* in Philadelphia, was invited and expected, but was unable to be present and sent, with his apology for his absence, the following lines :

HOW MARY GREW.

With wisdom far beyond her years,
And graver than her wondering peers,
So strong, so mild, combining still
The tender heart and queenly will,
To conscience and to duty true,
So, up from childhood, Mary Grew!

Then, in her gracious womanhood
She gave her days to doing good.
She dared the scornful laugh of men,
The hounding mob, the slanderer's pen.
She did the work she found to do,
A Christian heroine, Mary Grew!

The freed slave thanks her; blessing comes
To her from women's weary homes.
The wronged and erring find in her
Their censor mild and comforter.
The world were safe if but a few
Could grow in grace as Mary Grew!

So, New Year's Eve, I sit and say,
By this low wood-fire, ashen gray;
Just wishing, as the night shuts down,
That I could hear in Boston town,
In pleasant Chestnut Avenue,
From her own lips how Mary Grew!

And hear her graceful hostess tell
The silver voicéd oracle
Who lately through her parlors spoke
As through Dodona's sacred oak,
A wiser truth than any told
By Sappho's lips of ruddy gold,—
The way to make the world anew,
Is just to grow—as Mary Grew!

In response to an invitation to another of these Club gatherings, at which Lucretia Mott, and Mary Carpenter, of England, were to be present, and which he was unable to attend, Whittier wrote the following:

AMESBURY, Wednesday Eve.

MY DEAR MRS. SARGENT:

Few stronger inducements could be held out to me than that in thy invitation to meet Lucretia Mott and Mary Carpenter. But I do not see that I can possibly go to Boston this week. None the less do I thank thee, my dear friend, for thinking of me in connection with this visit.

My love to Lucretia Mott, and tell her I have never forgotten the kind welcome and generous sympathy she gave the young abolitionist at a time when he found small favor with his "orthodox" brethren. What a change she and I have lived to see! I hope to meet Miss Carpenter before she leaves us. For this and all thy kindness in times past, believe me gratefully,

Thy friend,
JOHN G. WHITTIER.

On still another occasion we were guests of the Sargents, with Whittier, at a social tea, when Robert Dale Owen was also present, with Mrs. Mattie Griffith Browne, and a few others, and the subject of spiritualism was under consideration—a subject in which Mr. Owen was greatly interested, and in which he was desirous especially of interesting Whittier. It was at a time when the alleged "materialization" of spirits was claiming much attention. Mr. Owen gave us an account of his own experience, and of some very remarkable spirit appearances. Whittier listened to his friend attentively, but inclined to be incredulous and skeptical, with every now and then an alert query: "Is thee sure there was no door here, and no opening there?" Of course he had no doubt as to immortality itself. In "Snow Bound" he affirms:

> " Yet Love will dream, and Faith will trust,
> (Since He who knows our need is just,)
> That somehow, somewhere, meet we must.
> Alas for him who never sees
> The stars shine through his cypress trees!
> Who, hopeless, lays his dead away,
> Nor looks to see the breaking day
> Across the mournful marbles play!
> Who have not learned, in hours of faith,
> The truth to flesh and sense unknown,
> That Life is ever lord of Death,
> And Love can never lose its own!"

It was as the Abolitionist and Poet that Whittier was most widely known to the general public. But his was an influential voice also in behalf of peace, temperance, the enfranchisement of women, prison reform and many humane interests. He was also an able, vigorous prose writer. His first important pamphlet, in 1833, which was entitled, "Justice and Expediency; or Slavery Considered with a view to its Rightful and

CHARLES SUMNER.

Effectual Remedy, Abolition," cost him nearly a year's earnings to print and distribute, besides the labor of its preparation. It was with a wisdom born of his own experience that, late in life, he counselled a young man who sought his advice: " Ally thyself early with some great cause."

Throughout his own life it was pre-eminently his aim

—" to render less
The sum of human wretchedness."

I was in the way of meeting Charles Sumner from time to time, and very pleasantly, in New York and Washington, during the latter part of my anti-slavery labors. I had the pleasure of sending him many petitions in behalf of his Personal Liberty measures in the Senate, a co-operation which he seemed much to appreciate. In his journeying to and fro between Boston and Washington I had occasional calls from him at the office of the *National Anti-Slavery Standard.* It was my privilege to pass with him, by appointment, in his own house, in Washington, now a part of the Arlington Hotel, the last evening before he was prostrated by an illness which soon culminated in his death.

He told me during our conversation that evening that it was his purpose, after his then pending measures in the interest of the colored people were disposed of, to devote the remainder of his public life to the promotion of International Arbitration. In his great lecture, entitled "The Duel between France and Germany," at the time of the Franco-Prussian war, which he delivered to immense audiences in Boston, and elsewhere, which I had the pleasure of hearing in New York, and which was subsequently published in a pamphlet still of great value for present use, he made a masterly plea for disarmament and the reduction of national armies to the standard only of ordinary police requirement. He declared : " An army is a despotism ; military service is a bondage ; nor can the passion for arms be reconciled with a true civilization ; " and, again : " Let the war system be abolished, and, in the glory of this consummation, how vulgar all that comes from battle! * * * Add peace to liberty,

"And with that virtue every virtue lives."

The day following my last evening with him, he was in his seat in the United States Senate, his last in that body, but he took no public part in its proceedings, beyond his sonorous "aye," given on a yea and nay vote for a bill introduced at my own request, in behalf of the National Temperance Society, to provide for a National Commission of Inquiry concerning the Alcoholic Liquor Traffic. That "aye" for my measure proved to be his last official, public word in the Senate.

The college mate and life long friend of Wendell Phillips, though he never joined the abolitionists as one of them, he was always in co-operative relations with them in his private and public life, and used playfully to boast that he was a year ahead of Mr. Phillips in subscribing for Mr. Garrison's *Liberator*.

Lydia Maria Child was the very intimate friend of both Whittier and Sumner, as also of Garrison and Phillips. She was another also who brought to the service of the anti-slavery movement a rare type of intellectual culture and ability, and who sacrificed a brilliant literary reputation upon the altar of the slave's redemption. I did not know her personally in the earlier period, at the time of her greatest anti-slavery activity, but occasionally met her, and her beloved and honored husband, David Lee Child, during the latter years of the conflict. I was especially grateful to her for very kind and helpful co-operation during my editorship of the *National Anti-Slavery Standard*, to which she made valuable contributions, sometimes over her own name and sometimes impersonal. Meanwhile she was doing her household work with her own hands. On one occasion she wrote :

Friend Powell:

I am afraid you have been thinking I have forgotten *The Standard*. But it is not so. I have

L. Maria Child.

been half crazed and excessively tired with house-cleaning and repairing, without any one to help my two old hands; everybody but myself being too genteel to work in these days.

Yours truly,
L. M. CHILD.

At another time she wrote :

"I have been intending for some weeks to send you an article, but I have been much hurried with spring work; and, to tell the truth, I do above all things, hate to write. I had rather wash, scour, do *any* thing, than to touch a pen."

In another letter accompanying an article for *The Standard*, she said :

" I have also written a paragraph for *The Independent* entitled "The Importance of One Vote," which you can copy, if you think it worth while to pull so small a string for Grant's election.

" To tell you the truth, I am scared half to death for fear those re-constructed States will make Seymour President."

Her three volumes, entitled "Progress of Religious Ideas," are a contribution to historical religious literature, of permanent value

Friend Powell,

My "bark is always worse than my bite." Mr. Child says so, and if _he_ don't know, who can?

I have been intending for some weeks to send you an article, but I have been much hurried with Spring-work; and, to tell the truth, I do, above all things, hate to write. I had rather wash, scour, do _anything_, than to touch a pen.

Yours truly,

L. M. Child.

representing profound thought and immense research.

These suggestive sentences are from her letters :

" The God *within* us is the God we really believe in, whatever we may have learned in catechisms and creeds."

.*.

" The outward is but a seeming and a show; the inward alone is permanent and real."

.*.

" In our pitiful anxiety how we shall appear before men, we forget how we appear before angels."

She left precise directions as to her funeral, that it should be private and inexpensive, and that she should be laid beside her " dear old mate," with whom, as she said to ———— she " did so long to have a talk it seemed as though she could not wait."

She directed these words to be put on her gravestone :

" You call us dead; we are not dead; we are only truly living now."

MEMORANDA OF THE UNWRITTEN CHAPTERS.

———

[IN the memoranda left, the unwritten chapters are not even sketched. But it seems due to the writer's generous purpose, that this barely hinted outline should be given, of work and workers for Temperance; for the Indians; for Prison Reform; for the Equal Rights of Women; for Peace and Arbitration; and in behalf of Purity.]

Emerson, John Brown, George L. Stearns, George W. Julian, Rev. Samuel May, Lucy Stone, Rev. Antoinette Brown Blackwell, Gerrit Smith, Frederick Douglass, Rev. Beriah Green, Parker Pillsbury, Charles C. Burleigh, Oliver Johnson, Giles B. Stebbins.

———

Julia Ward Howe, Mary A. Livermore, Abby Hopper Gibbons, Elizabeth Gay, Dr. Elizabeth Blackwell, Dr. Emily Blackwell, Louisa M. Alcott.

National Standard 1872.   Indian Civilization—Journey to San Francisco—Chicago Fire—Barclay White—Chinese.

First Trip to Europe 1873—International Prison Congress.   Drink Episode—Cardinal Manning—Mr. Raper and Mr. Barker, Sir Wilfred Lawson and Exeter Hall.   Continental Trip—Mrs. Butler—Liverpool.

Standard and *National Temperance Advocate*, Editorship and Secretary.   Wm. E. Dodge, J. N. Stearns, Gen. Neal Dow, Dr. Cuyler, Miss Willard, Dr. Richardson, Dr. Lees, Mr. Rae, Mrs. Lucas. Congress, Commission of Inquiry, Senator Frye, Mr. Dingley, Joseph D. Taylor.   National Prohibitory Amendment.   Canon Wilberforce, Archbishop Farrar, Gen. Fisk, Ramabai.

New York Committee State Regulation of Vice. H. J. Wilson, M. P., and Rev. J. P. Gledstone. Second European Trip 1877—First International Congress and Federation.   Canon and Mrs. Butler, Mr. Stansfeld, Sir Harcourt Johnstone, Prof. Stuart, Prof. Humbert, M. Henri Pierson, Madame De Morsier, Mme. De Gingins, George Gillet, Henry Richard, Maria Richardson.   Reformation Hall—Mrs. Butler, Eliza Wigham and Mrs. Howe, Dr. Blackwell.

Third European Trip 1883.—The Hague. Mrs. Butler, Count and Countess Hogendorp, Madame Klerck. Socialism—the King—Motley Palace.

Fourth European Trip—Fourth International Congress—London 1886. Mr. Stead, M. De Laveleye. Toynbee Hall—Dr. Nevins, Mr. Minod.

Fifth European Trip—Fifth Congress, Geneva 1889. Paris Exposition—Absence of Mrs. Butler. Canon Butler died March 14, 1890, in his 71st year. Mrs. Ballington Booth and the Servia.

Sixth European Trip—Sixth Triennial Congress —1891 at Brussels, Belgium. Mrs. Butler and others.

World's Congress on Social Purity. Chicago— Archbishop Ireland, Mr. Gerry, Father Cleary, Judge Bonney, Mr. De Watteville, Mrs. Livermore, Rev. Anna Garlin Spencer.

Seventh European Trip—London, July 1894— Rosebery, Salisbury, Devonshire, etc.

National Purity Congress, Baltimore, Md., October, 1895 — First National — Characterize.

Rev. Dr. McVickar, Rev. Dr. Lewis, Dr. Emily and Dr. Elizabeth Blackwell—Woman's Medical College, Rev. Dr. Sabine, Dr. J. H. Kellogg and others.

Eighth European Trip—Congress at Berne, 1896. Birmingham Conference. Visit at the Clarks' at Street—John Bright.

Ninth European Trip—London 1898—International Congress. Social Purity Alliance. Archdeacon of London. National Vigilance Association. Mr. Stead. Canon Rawnsley, English Lakes.

This form laid low, in beautiful ripe manliness?
This deep-toned, gentle voice with sweet com-
    pelling power to persuade
  Hushed from its labor?
This matchless tact, grown strong by love and
    service,
Yet fine and sensitive to handle God's most
    delicate work
  Lost to humanity's cause?
This gentleness and courage so nobly joined, they
    seemed a seamless garment
Worn with all dignity and kindliness—
All these rich, ripe graces lost to God's service?
    Not so!   In other, fairer fields he still shall
    serve.
    Our Father!   We question not thy wisdom
    and thy love;
We only plead, "Anoint unto thy service here
Others thy servants,
With a like strength, fidelity, and untiring love."

ANNA CANBY JANNEY.

AARON M. POWELL.

ANNA RICE POWELL.

WITH the message of assured faith in the soul's continued life, which was left by Lydia Maria Child for record upon her tombstone, my brother laid down his pen, for a temporary absence in Philadelphia, to attend the Yearly Meeting of the Religious Society of Friends, held at Fifteenth and Race Streets. They were the last words of his writing in this volume. If he had been permitted to choose "last words"—words to be imprinted with the indelible touch that only death's seal can give, perhaps there are no words that could have spoken more directly to the hearts of those sore-stricken by his departure. For they know that for him to "truly live" is to pour out his heart of love, not only upon those nearest and dearest to him, but upon the work also to which he had felt himself called. They may well believe that, if it be given to the liberated spirit not only to enter

into the joys of the faithful, but to be faithful
still to all its past, then he will still minister
to his own, and will labor on in the fields
where laborers are few.

On the morning of Seventh day, Fifth
month, 13, 1899, with his wife, Anna Rice
Powell, he left his home in Plainfield, N. J.,
and arrived in Philadelphia in time for a part
only of the morning session of the meeting
of Ministers and Elders. The intermission
between the morning and the afternoon
sessions, was spent in happy intercourse with
their sister, planning, among other things, for
a quiet opportunity to read together the
finished chapters of the "Reminiscences."
He remarked "I shall have to go slowly this
week ;" and yet, he seemed not less vigorous
than at any time during the last two years—
years really of unacknowledged invalidism.
When it was time for the afternoon session
to begin, they returned to the meeting house,
where he was invited to a seat with ministering Friends. He left his wife and sister with
the words "I am sorry to be separated from

you two!" Near the close of the meeting, during which, there had been much expression of unity with the presence by courtesy, of Friends from the far West and from England, he rose and said: "It has been very gratifying to me to observe in the portion of the morning session which I was privileged to attend, and again this afternoon, the tendency to a spirit of unification among Friends. We each have to live a life"—He ceased speaking, and was observed to be falling forward. A friend facing him and near him, instantly supported him; and hands as kind as brothers' hands could be, laid him upon the seat from which he had risen, and used every means for his restoration. A physician present in the meeting, pronounced further efforts unavailing,—the spirit had departed. The solemn silence was presently broken by the concluding minute of the clerk; and Friends quietly passed away from the meeting house.

The body rested until Second day morning, in the home of Samuel and Sarah Ash whose hospitality he had many times enjoyed. On

First day evening, a few friends gathered about the beloved form whose face, beautiful to look upon, seemed to have the light of the Heavenly life upon it. One and another of the dear friends, those of his own generation, and others—young men and women spoke words of love; and told how this life had entered into their own, and opened noble ideals to them, and urged to their attainment. That the *young* should bear testimony that he had been teacher and guide to them; and should pledge themselves to his unfinished work,—what sweeter compensation could there be, for a life of unselfish service!

On the following day the journey was made to Ghent, New York, the old home in the Hudson River Valley, now the home of the younger brother, George T. Powell. On Third day afternoon, relatives, friends and neighbors gathered at the homestead for the funeral service. Among the Friends present, of the New York Yearly Meeting, were Robert S. Haviland, Charles M. Robinson, William and Anna Jackson, John William

Hutchinson, Elias Underhill, Tacie P. Willets, Henry Wilbur and Franklin T. Carpenter. Of the Philadelphia Yearly Meeting, Mary Travilla and Isaac Roberts were in attendance. Tender words of prayer and thanksgiving were spoken, and again, loving testimony was borne to the purity and faithfulness and stimulating power of the life just passed from our sight. Henry G. Adams of Plainfield, N. J., spoke in behalf, not only of the Friends of Plainfield whose meeting will miss the helpful presence, but for the city mourning the loss of a valued citizen.

Isaac Roberts said in part :

" If the great purpose of life is the development of character through noble service, then how can any life be more successful than his has been?   If, as has been well said, ' there is but one failure, and that is, not to be true to the best one knows,' then success must be found in fidelity to the Truth as revealed to him.   If the fellowship of great work, the companionship of noble thoughts, the consciousness of effective work in great causes, if these constitute happiness, how truly happy his life has been.   If quiet contentment, peace, and full soul-communion in the home life; if silent communion with the Holy Spirit both in work and worship,—if these constitute blessedness, how truly blessed his life has been, and how confident we may be that life has simply known transition, a happy change from loving service here, to higher, holier service in the life beyond, 'the life that is life indeed.'

"As we contemplate the life and character of our friend so lately with us, now so greatly blessed, the thought that Whittier expressed in contemplating the life and character of John Woolman comes before us; we have 'felt awed and solemnized by the presence of a serene and beautiful spirit, redeemed of the Lord from all selfishness, and we have been made grateful for the ability to recognize and the disposition to love him;' and we recall, too, the words which our Quaker poet addressed to one of his well known friends, who, like our friend, was blessed by a quick translation from work to reward:

> " As a guest who may not stay
> Long and sad farewells to say,
> Glides with smiling face away,
>
> Of the sweetness and the zest,
> Of thy happy life possessed,
> Thou hast left us at thy best.
>
> Now that thou hast gone away,
> What remains of one to say
> Who was open as the day ?

Safe thou art on every side,
Friendship nothing finds to hide,
Love's demand is satisfied.

Keep for us, dear friend, where'er
Thou art waiting, all that here
Made thy earthly presence dear.

And when fall our feet, as fell
Thine, upon the asphodel,
Let thy dear smile greet us well;

Proving in a world of bliss
All we fondly dream in this,—
Love is one with holiness !"

The form was laid away in the burial ground of the Friends at Ghent, beside the little daughter early deceased, and near his parents Townsend and Catharine Macy Powell. A noble oak shelters these graves ; the " everlasting hills " are about them, and the quiet of that beautiful country.

While the funeral service was in progress at Ghent, in Philadelphia the Purity Alliance of that city was holding a memorial meeting in place of the conference appointed for that hour, at which my brother had promised his willingness to speak, assuring the secretary that it would be "for no other compensation than the joy of doing good." Other memorial meetings were held by the Philanthropic Committee of the New York Yearly Meeting, and by the Friends of his own meeting in Plainfield. In these meetings were testimonies tender and true, from his fellow workers in many fields, and in different religious denominations, to the success of the unselfish life.

His birth-place was Clinton, Dutchess County, N. Y. In 1845, when he was thirteen years old, his parents removed to Ghent, to the farm-home of his mother's girlhood. He had the customary life of country boys in those days, of farm work in the summer, and a few months in the public school in the winter. But he was blessed with that best inheritance, a hungering and thirsting mind, and the eyes that see. That retired farming life was in the midst of great natural beauty, with wooded hills close at hand, and beyond a fertile valley the outline of the beautiful blue Catskills thirty miles away, along the western horizon. It might be said of him, as of Wordsworth, "Fair seed time had his soul," in that season of close intimacy with nature, that life of labor simple and sincere. The few books of those early years were made to yield their utmost treasure to him. It was a life very free from incident—no record of travel, nor of social gaiety, nor exciting recreation; only the kindly intercourse of a Friendly neighborhood to alternate with the exactions of daily toil. Even then, he was not living to himself alone. He had taken into close companionship his only sister, enough younger than himself to receive from him almost fatherly care. His own high ideals of life and duty, his glimpses of spiritual things—he shared them all with her. He became her guide; literally the light of her young life; the object of her passionate devotion. Although she could only follow him afar, it was he who gave the direction to her life. Some "accents of the Holy Ghost" early found their way to his soul, and set vibrating the chords of aspiration toward all that is best in life,—chords that never ceased to respond to the touch of the Most High.

His own record has told how he was moved by the appeals for help when there were few to help in the labors of the abolitionists. He has himself related how the visit of Stephen and Abby Kelley Foster took him away from this quiet country life ; away from his cherished plans for college education into the arduous missionary life of the anti-slavery apostles. This was in 1851. The next ten years were given almost wholly to public service in the anti-slavery cause. In April of 1861 the Ghent home was the happy scene of his marriage with Judith Anna Rice of Worcester, Mass. As Miss Rice was not then in membership with the Religious Society of Friends, the laws of Massachusetts did not admit of their using the marriage ceremony of Friends. For this reason the marriage was celebrated at Ghent. In the summer of 1863 the mob spirit was rampant in New York City. This was the summer in

AARON M. POWELL,
AT THE AGE OF 17, AND HIS SISTER.

which the house of James and Abby Hopper Gibbons was attacked by an angry "copperhead" mob, because it was thought to be the home of Horace Greeley; and furniture, books and clothing all destroyed. The same spirit more or less infected the country. My brother was the conspicuous object of "copperhead" hatred in the Hudson River Valley; and the discovered plotting against his life made it seem wise for himself and his wife to leave Ghent for a time.

In February of 1864 another happy tie was formed with the old home, in the birth of their daughter Lizzie Rice Powell. But the claims of the anti-slavery work were still strong upon him, and New York City became their residence, to be exchanged in 1880 for Plainfield, New Jersey. His marriage was a relation in which his joys were multiplied, his anxieties divided—a relation which brought him sympathetic companionship in all his labors. The mob spirit cannot prevail against a home whose law is love and co-operation; the man whose best ideals are shared by his wife is fortified for the most arduous work appointed to him. This was the blessedness of my brother's lot.

The death of their precious daughter just before the Christmas day of 1867, sweet sorrow though it was, with no drop of bitterness in it, was a very sore sorrow; and for a time it seemed that in her death all joy had died. One whose heart was wrapped up in the little girl, writing of her in 1866, said:

"How I wish you could see her, she is so lovely! Her golden hair, blue eyes, fair skin and pink cheeks, make her as pretty as a little girl can be, and her ways are very charming. The mother instinct is strongly developed in her; and she is happy with her baby, be it handkerchief, shawl or dolly."

And again in January, 1868:

"Did I write of the sweet visit I had with her in October? It was one of those weeks of perfect weather, and she was out with me a good deal. One day we were on Broadway, and she held my finger and led me at 'her own sweet will;' and at every window of toys or pictures we stopped to gaze as long as she wished. Passers by turned to look again at her radiant little face. It was the first time I had realized that she was growing up to be a companion for me; and I was so proud and happy that day, that she almost belonged to me!"

The sorely stricken parents bowed to the wave of sorrow as it passed over them; then rose up to do, in patience and trust, the work given them to do. The ministry of love that could not pour itself out upon the sweet, invisible presence with them all these years, has been the blessing of many a young soul struggling with the problems of life; and the childless home has been made a place of helpful and happy resort for the young.

One young man to whom my brother's heart was closely drawn by kindred interests, sends the message:

"There are very few men for whom I had as warm a personal affection. He was so young in his sympathies that we felt he was a real comrade; and a comrade whose presence and association was an inspiring incentive to all that was best in us."

Another, with whom he has had intimate business relations, writes:

"All his friends will share in my grief, since all who knew him must have loved him. He was indeed a man whose upright life and pure character challenged the admiration of all. To me he has been conspicuously a model upon which I sought to mould my own actions."

The nineteen busy years lived in Plainfield have had much happiness in them. Residence in New York for a period of fifteen years gave very keen zest to the satisfaction of coming into ownership of a modest home in the embowered city of Plainfield. He felt that it added years to his life among us, that he could leave the towering walls and the ceaseless stir and pressure of the great metropolis; and after a comfortable railroad journey of three-quarters of an hour, with the refreshment in summer of the ferry, and the ever changing beauty of the bay, come to the quiet of his own home. Green grass and lily of the valley, and cherry tree and maples never ministered of their freshness, fragrance and shadows to more grateful appreciation. And more than this: the strangers found themselves warmly welcomed to the congenial company of Friends whose meetings in the ancient meeting house (1788) on Watchung Avenue it was their pleasure to attend and support with their co-operation. The Young Friends' Association of this Meeting would bear testimony that my brother's help to them has been such as not to leave them helpless now he is gone; but such as to call out their own power to do, and to go forward. Most pleasant social relations with their townspeople were soon established. Their contribution to the social life of Plainfield is suggested in the following letter from one of their young friends:

"I associate you and Mr. Powell with so much that has been happy and inspiring in my life. How often I have looked back to the cosy evenings at your house when you invited some interesting personality from the great world (Miss Dodge and others), and then shared the pleasure with as many others as your little home would accommodate. You don't know how many times I have thought of, and spoken of those evenings to my friends, as, to me, the ideal of hospitality—the privilege of bringing people together under conditions which would help to make life broader and nobler for them;

and you and Mr. Powell receiving so cordially, putting every guest at ease and making the occasion one of rare privilege. That is the way in which I think oftenest of you and Mr. Powell; though I know these were but the relaxations of a life of noble, unselfish endeavor. I think too of the interest you both took in all the young life of Plainfield, sharing our pleasures with keenest sympathy, and I know there are now many of us who belonged to the younger set, as well as those of a later day, who think of you with loving sympathy, and of Mr. Powell's beautiful life with gratitude."

His active co-operation was given, as far as the limitations of health allowed, to the varied interests of the town. Sometimes his helping hand was needed in the formation of a Boys' Club; again he would be asked to serve on the committee of award of the medal for the best essay writing in the High School. The workers for Temperance, and the struggling Woman's Suffrage Club had such help from him as his physical strength permitted. A most kind recognition of his work is given in the following extract from a letter from a committee of the Plainfield Ministers' Association, signed by Rev. E. M. Rodman, Rev. D. J. Yerkes and Rev. Wm. R. Richards :

"In carrying out the duty assigned us, we desire to make note of our sincere admiration of the life and work of Mr. Powell, which made him so well known and so justly esteemed in this country and in every land where the friends of God and of man are laboring for the betterment of mankind. Every association of such laborers sought, and never sought in vain, your husband's assistance."

Another member of this Association, Rev. A. H. Lewis, who had united with him in much personal service in the work for Purity, writes in a private letter :

"The loss to me, personally, is almost as keen as though he had been my brother, after the flesh. If my engagements could be put aside, in justice to my public work, I would be at the burial; and yet Aaron is not buried. The house in which he lived has fallen; he has entered into the 'house not made with hands.' This I know. It must be that we go hence and leave the work which God has given us; but in his case I do not see who can take the work he leaves. * * * His life is already a permanent factor in the spiritual history of the world, nay, of the universe. What he has done for right and righteousness can never be undone, and in the not too far off home coming there will be found over against his name on the records, such numberless things done for God, and humanity, and truth, and justice, and righteousness and purity, as this world has not been able to understand, much less to appreciate."

The last Sabbath in the unbroken home was gladdened by the company of a party of young friends from New York. One of these writes :

"My last picture is of the two, so truly one in spirit, as they stood on the porch of their hospitable home, and waved that sweet adieu that seemed to us a benediction. I can never forget those two happy, helpful days."

It became the motive of my brother's life to make better conditions for the young; to be a co-worker with God for the welfare of his little children. After negro slavery was legally abolished, he devoted himself for twenty-one years to editorial work upon the *National Temperance Advocate*, and in response to many appeals for public service in this cause. The labors of Mrs. Butler and her associates

were early brought to his notice. This work
for the safety of the young, both young men
and maidens, touched the very tenderest
chords of his soul. Here again were "fields
white for the harvest" with few laborers to
take up the painful, difficult task. Here were
"New Abolitionists" appealing to him for
help. He made their cause his own, and the
last years of his life were given up to it with
complete consecration.

The writing of these Reminiscences was
undertaken during the last year, at the repeated suggestion of friends who felt that
there must be much of permanent interest
and value in the recollections of such a life,
intimately associated as it had been with men
and women who left their impress upon their
times, and devoted as it had been to the
furtherance of great reforms. As my brother
progressed with the writing, he found it most
interesting and absorbing. There was much
in the retrospect that was of necessity sad-
dening; but there was also the glow of
enthusiasm awakened by living again, in

memory, with the great souls whom he has pictured with sincere and sympathetic hand. The record of the labors of the past, looked at for the first time, as a whole, was a surprise to him. And he loved to bear the testimony, as many others have done, that whatever he had been able to do for the anti-slavery cause, it had done immeasurably more for him! More than once he remarked, "I hope I shall live to finish this book!" This was not to be. The part he has written covers hardly more than half his years. It is deeply to be regretted that we cannot have from his own hand the history of the three decades that he has barely touched upon; and the recognition that it was in his heart to give, of the invaluable services of his co-workers.

It is not possible to give any adequate summary of my brother's work in the Temperance cause. "Twenty-one years of editorial work" can hardly convey to those not experienced in this exacting calling, an idea of its demands. Nor can any complete record be given of his public speaking on this subject, in this country and in England. Very few manuscript addresses are left, because it was his method to prepare an outline of the thought to be presented, with only the heads for reference in speaking. At a public welcome extended to him in 1883 by a committee of the London Auxiliary of the United Kingdom Alliance for the Legislative Suppression of the Liquor Traffic, the following resolution was moved by the Rev. Dr. Burns:

"That this meeting of Temperance Reformers, assembled on the invitation of the committee of the London Auxiliary of the Alliance, hereby extends a cordial and fraternal welcome to A. M. Powell, Esq., and Mrs. Powell, of New York, whose temperance work in the United States they desire to recognize with high regard and approbation; and they further avail themselves of this occasion to convey, through Mr. Powell, to the American National Temperance Society an expression of their deep and growing interest in the progress of temperance reform in every part of that great Republic to which the world is indebted for the origin of the temperance movement of modern times.

"Mr. Robert Rae, of the National Temperance League, was asked to support the resolution. He said he knew somewhat of the temperance work of Mr. Powell on the other side of the Atlantic. Mr.

Powell was an all-round man, and there was no gentleman he met when he was in America two years ago who seemed to him to possess such a thorough knowledge of the position of the temperance movement all over the United States, and he might add, all over the world. He (Mr. Rae) was surprised to find he understood so thoroughly what we were doing on this side of the water. We often had occasion to consult him about temperance in the United States and never found him wanting in information upon any such point."

He has referred to his last interview with Senator Sumner in regard to securing a Congressional Commission of Inquiry in which he was deeply interested. He was called to Washington many times to appear before the committees having this subject in charge. His concern that the temperance question should have broadest and most statesmanlike consideration is expressed in the closing words of one of his public addresses:

"The temperance reform has many phases. Each is important. Its national aspect is fundamental. The sovereignty of the nation is supreme. For state, municipal, and local temperance progress, it is of vital moment that the national revenue copartnership with brewers, distillers, and liquor sellers be dissolved. While the 'rumseller' is the subject of common denunciation, it must be borne in mind that the consenting citizen, under the national, as under the state governments, must needs share his responsibility for the evil traffic.

"To achieve ultimate complete success, temperance work must be not only thorough in detail, but comprehensive in its scope. Its magnitude, in all its aspects, is indeed great, but with God's blessing and the fidelity of philanthropic, Christian men and women, it is destined to triumph, our beloved country to be rescued from the destructive plague of alcoholism, the nation to stand forth redeemed, regenerated and disenthralled."

He visited Europe for the first time in the summer of 1872. He was appointed by the National Committee of the United States, a member of the International Prison Congress held in London ; and he was also the bearer of a memorial adopted by the Representative Committee of the New York Yearly Meeting of Friends, upon the subject of Capital Punishment. He was accompanied by Aaron C. Macy of Hudson, N. Y., the uncle whose name he bears. Writing in a private letter of this Congress, he says :

"The International Prison Congress has finished its labors, and adjourned an hour ago. (July 13, 1872.) What it has done, has been as a whole, very well done, as you will see by the summary of propositions which I will send you a steamer later. But on Intemperance, as related to crime and the death penalty, it has been wholly inadequate. I have to-day had in the Congress, what in anti-slavery days would have been termed a 'real fight' to get the Congress to prolong its sessions two days, and discuss properly those two vital subjects. I did not expect to accomplish it, but I did succeed in placing upon the managers the responsibility of declining to entertain those topics."

Three days later he adds concerning this episode :

"My effort was not in vain. I am assured that what I said was felt by all, and sympathized with by many. I received yesterday a special invitation to visit this evening Archbishop Manning, the most distinguished Archbishop of London (Roman Catholic), who was present in the Congress during my effort. He is much interested in the temperance efforts now in progress here, and I shall go for the interview which he invites for this evening."

His testimony in the Prison Congress concerning the relation of Intemperance to crime brought him many invitations to speak upon Temperance,—among them an invitation to be one of the speakers with Rev. Theodore Cuyler and others at a "Temperance Breakfast" at the Crystal Palace, at which he was present. While the Prison Congress was in session, he assisted also at a meeting of the World's Peace Congress, called by Mrs. Julia Ward Howe, and presided over by Lady Bowring. And it was during this stay in London that he first attended a meeting on Purity.

The special mission accomplished, of this visit to London, there followed several weeks of pure recreation, in journeying with our uncle through Switzerland and France, and in visiting many interesting and picturesque parts of Great Britain. The congenial companionship, and the thrilling interest of the new Old World made this a memorable summer in my brother's experience. He did not foresee that it was the first of many pilgrimages, the opening of new fields of labor, and the beginning of friendships that were for all time.

His active co-operation with Mrs. Butler and her co-workers may be said to date from the visit of Henry J. Wilson, Esq., and Rev. J. P. Gledstone in the summer of 1876. In a letter written at the instance of Mrs. Butler they are thus introduced:

"Mrs. Butler, who is at present overwhelmed with engagements, has desired me to write to you in her name on behalf of the British Continental and General Federation, in reference to the trans-atlantic mission upon which it has been resolved to enter, for the sake of mutual aid and encouragement in the prosecution of our common cause, of which you are, I believe, already informed. The two gentlemen who have been selected by the Executive Committee of the Federation for the work of this mission, namely, Henry J. Wilson, Esq., of Sheffield, and the Rev. J. P. Gledstone, a Congregationalist minister of London, have now finally arranged (D. V.) to sail from Liverpool on Thursday, the 13th April prox., directing their course in the first instance to New York. You would be conferring a great favor on these gentlemen and on the great International organization from whom they derive their credentials if you could kindly furnish them with letters of introduc-

tion to any persons—whether ladies or gentlemen—
who might be likely to further their object. * * '
It is essential that the two delegates should be as
definitely and fully informed as possible, immediately upon their arrival, upon points calculated
to shape their course in America, as to which they
have naturally been unable to form any decided plan
beforehand. * * * Our work upon the continent
of Europe has already made great progress; and
we are therefore the more anxious to stretch out,
and to grasp the right hand of fellowship with
those to whom we are bound not only by the.
interests of a common cause, but by the ties of
consanguinity."

Very shortly after the arrival of Mr. Wilson
(later, Member of Parliament) and Rev. Mr.
Gledstone, invitations were sent out in the
name of a committee, whose chairman was
Mrs. Abby Hopper Gibbons, for a private
conference and reception to these gentlemen,
in the parlors of the New York Infirmary.
A similar conference and reception was held
a month later in the parlors of the Isaac T.
Hopper home. The committee improvised
at that time to further their work, consisted
of Mrs. Abby Hopper Gibbons, Emily Blackwell, M. D., Mrs. Elizabeth Gay, Aaron M.

Powell, Mrs. Cornelia C. Hussey, Anna Lukens, M. D., William H. Hussey and Mrs. Anna Rice Powell. This committee regarded itself as a temporary organization for just that service. But it proved quite otherwise. The history of the work in England brought to light the fact that need for similar work existed here. In the following September the committee addressed a letter to Mrs. Josephine E. Butler, secretary of the British and General Federation, in relation to the late visit of Mr. Wilson and Mr. Gledstone; and in reference to the efforts being made here to introduce the European System of Regulation. Brief extracts are given from this letter:

"We improve the occasion of our first meeting, as a committee, since the departure of Messrs. Wilson and Gledstone, to communicate to you, and through you to your philanthropic co-workers, our grateful appreciation of the timely and important labors of those gentlemen in this and other cities of the United States. Their work here has attested their eminent fitness for the mission to which they were deputed, and their coming was singularly opportune. They have inaugurated a movement which is destined to extend, and ultimately to embrace the whole country, and, we trust, not only to prevent the introduction of the license system here, but to become auxiliary to its destruction wherever it may prevail in other lands. * * * Our committee is as yet but 'provisional' in its character, but we trust in due time to win accessions to our numbers and strength, and to be able to co-operate, both heartily and efficiently, as an auxiliary of your International Association. A chief element of weakness and danger here is the over confidence of the many, who have given little thought to the subject, and who do not understand the stealthy tactics of the license advocates. *.* * The special danger is in covert and apparently innocent measures to carry out ulterior, immoral purposes. We shall vigilantly watch and seek resolutely to thwart all such evil designs."

It proved a long labor upon which the committee had entered. "To vigilantly watch, and to seek resolutely to thwart all evil designs" of the legislators, allowed no release from their efforts. The need for work which they had but dimly guessed in the beginning, became more and more apparent with further investigation of the laws. Having "put his hand to the plow," there not only was no turning back for my brother, but his concern deepened as the years went by.

One of his most cherished memories was of Abby Hopper Gibbons, for many years chairman of the New York Committee. Born to philanthropic labor, as the daughter of Isaac T. Hopper, her life was given to efforts for ameliorating the conditions of the poor, and of the outcast. My brother had great pleasure in Louisa M. Alcott's lively portraiture of Mrs. Gibbons in the following letter after a Christmas day with her at Randall's Island, by his arrangement :

Dec. 25th, 1875.

DEAR MRS. POWELL:

I have had such an interesting day that I must tell you how much I enjoyed it, and regretted that you couldn't "go halves."

The fog did not daunt me, and I found Mrs. G. on the boat without any trouble. I lost my heart to the dear little lady in five minutes, for she gave the Mayor and Commissioner —— such a splendid lecture on pauperism and crime that the important gentlemen hadn't a leg to stand upon. I enjoyed it immensely; and the officials appeared no more.

The poor children welcomed her like the sun; and we spent the time in giving out toys and sweeties to the orphans, idiots and babies. It was pathetic yet beautiful to see their happiness as the friend of thirty years came among them, so motherly and sweet; and I am sure a sort of halo surrounded the little black bonnet as she led us from room to room like a Xmas good angel in a waterproof. * * *

Mr. Gibbons was very friendly; and the whole trip was a great success, being a different sort of day from any I ever spent before, as the only gifts I had were those I gave away, and my Xmas dinner the one I saw the poor things eat, minus spoons.

Mrs. G. will meet us at the Tombs next Wed., 11 A. M. Give her name and its all right. Hope you can go. Regards to "thy" husband, who I trust is better.

Truly yours,

L. M. A.

When at the age of ninety-one Mrs. Gibbons passed away, my brother wrote in *The Philanthropist :*

"Mrs. Gibbons engaged in the work of our committee with great earnestness, and with rare wisdom and tact born of large experience. Writing to one of her intimate committee associates of some new development, indicating the activity of the regulation propagandists, she says: ' It bids us be vigilant. The advocates of State Regulation are more numerous and vile than we supposed.'

Again she writes: 'If I were a few years younger I would meet them face to face at Albany.' In response to a suggestion, on one occasion, that in the prosecution of our work she be relieved of all possible burdens in connection therewith, she writes: 'Never suggest the word *burden* in any work in which I take so lively an interest.' Again she writes: 'Never fear *me*, dear friends; keep an eye on the work we have undertaken.' Again: 'I declare the indifference of those who ought to take an interest in this question amazes and vexes me.' * * * Great, indeed, is the sense of loss which her removal to the world beyond brings to those hitherto associated with her in the various phases of humane and Christian work to which her life was so unreservedly dedicated."

The first International Congress of the British Continental and General Federation was held in Geneva, Switzerland, in September of 1877. He was sent by the New York Committee as delegate. Mrs. Julia Ward Howe was also present; and in her account of the Congress in the *Woman's Journal*, she mentions that

"In one of the closing sessions, Aaron M. Powell, of New York, made a most interesting statement regarding the various attempts hitherto made to introduce into the United States, laws concerning regulation of vice."

He himself says in a private letter written from Geneva :

" This Congress (I am even more impressed than before I came) is to mark the beginning of an agitation which will extend much beyond the question merely of repeal and abolition of regulation statutes and machinery."

In June of 1883, Mrs. Butler's secretary wrote at her request :

"Mrs. Butler is quite unable to write to express her hope that you and Mrs. Powell will be present at the meeting at the Hague. She asks me to say how anxious she is that you should come, as it is especially desirable that there should be some powerful representative from America."

This Third International Congress, held at the Hague in the following September, my brother and his wife attended as delegates, and found it an occasion of very great interest. In a letter to the *Woman's Journal* at this time, he wrote :

"One is often reminded by it of the kindred experiences of American Abolitionists in their warfare against slavery. But slavery has disappeared, and the name of Garrison, once so abhorred, is now among the most honored. The pioneer in this great crusade for the emancipation of the white slave of State sanctioned vice is a woman. But this odious form of white slavery for the purposes of sexual debauchery is also doomed; with the emancipation of these most wronged and degraded of women will come a truer liberty for all women, an ennobling influence for all men, and the names of Mrs. Butler and her effective co-workers in this grand conflict, now frequently spoken of with derision and contempt, shall in due time be enrolled by a grateful people among the truest and noblest of the benefactors of mankind. The Federation appeals to America for sympathy and co-operation. May it not appeal in vain."

Other International Congresses were attended, in London 1886, Geneva 1889, Brussels 1891, London 1894, Berne 1896 and again in London 1898. At Berne, and twice in London, he was accompanied by his wife. With every recurring Congress came such earnest appeal from the European workers as this from Mrs. Butler:

"I write, not only for myself but on behalf of

our committee, to beg that you will make every reasonable effort to be with us, for we feel the necessity of having personal communication again with our American friends; and you will, I am sure, take back with you to New York a wonderful impression of the progress of our cause, and of the irresistible power with which our principles are rolling along and making their way in the midst even of other distressing political storms."

The attendance of the Congresses in England was always the occasion of more or less service in the Temperance cause; along with other study of social conditions. During the Congress of 1886 in London, an evening was spent at Toynbee Hall, of which he gives the following account in his editorial correspondence with *The Philanthropist:*

"Some of the foreign delegates, one evening during the progress of the Congress, were invited to dine, and given a reception, at Toynbee Hall, in the south of London, in the midst of its overcrowded poorer population. It is a practical democratic experiment, being made mainly by University young men, of whom Mr. George Butler is one, to live in the midst of these poor people, to fraternize with them, to study their condition and needs, and to share with them their own advantages of culture, by inviting them to lectures and conferences on a variety of subjects, amusements of various types, etc., etc., and thus to neutralize in some degree the evil results of the sharply defined class distinctions between the rich and cultured and the poorer classes of London. Toynbee Hall includes lodgings in which the young men reside as a temporary home, out of business hours, a large dining hall, a spacious drawing room, a lecture room, etc. The objects and methods of the experiment were happily explained by the Rev. Mr. Barnett, who presided at the dinner, and congratulatory responses were made in behalf of the guests by M. De Laveleye and Count Hogendorp, of the Hague.

Later in the evening two hundred or more of the workingmen of the vicinity were present at the reception, and in the lecture room were addressed by M. De Laveleye and Mr. Powell. The experiment is one of great interest, with the promise of a large measure of usefulness. It is not now, as we trust it ultimately may be, conducted upon a total abstinence temperance basis."

On my brother's return from the Brussels Congress in 1891, he took the opportunity while in London to call upon Archdeacon Farrar and Cardinal Manning to ask for papers for the World's Temperance Congress to be held in Chicago in 1893. Of these interesting interviews he writes in private letters :

"On Second day I called, with Mr. Raper, on Archdeacon Farrar, and we had a delightful interview with him.   He promises, with great cordiality, a paper for the World's Temperance Congress, and gives me as his topic, which we are at liberty to announce, 'The Awakening of the Universal Conscience to the Duty of Resisting the Curse of Drink.'   This is an exceedingly valuable addition to our list."

And again :

"Cardinal Manning received us most cordially, and will furnish the desired paper—his theme 'Total Abstinence.'   He is well along in the *eighties*, but his eye is bright and his mind very clear and quick.   When I thanked him for consenting to prepare the paper, he responded—'I shall do it with great joy.'   The interview, which covered a wide range of conversation, was one of much interest."

As the work in the anti-slavery cause had priceless compensation in intimate association with men and women consecrated to unselfish work, so his co-operation with the "New

Abolitionists " had the happy reward of close friendship with some of the noblest souls. The homes of the Wilsons of Sheffield, the Gledstones, and Rapers and Brownes of London, the Clarks of Street, the Richardsons of York, and the Martineaus of Birmingham were hospitably opened to him, and were sources of strength and inspiration. In *The Philanthropist* for October, 1889, he writes of an hour with Mrs. Butler who had been unable to attend the Congress in Geneva :

" Yesterday, the 20th, we journeyed from London to the quiet, beautiful old Cathedral town of Winchester, and had an hour with Canon and Mrs. Butler. Canon Butler is very feeble, but cherishes the faith that presently his strength will be again renewed. Serene in spirit, with good cheer, his presence was a benediction. Mrs. Butler seemed very frail in body, and though worn with the prolonged period of nursing and care of her beloved husband, which she can delegate to no one else, she is keenly alive to the interest to which her life has been so largely dedicated, and had watched from her quiet seclusion at the Close, the proceedings of the Congress at Geneva, of which she had been kept fully advised. Both Canon and Mrs. Butler spoke with much appreciation of the message of sympathetic remembrance telegraphed to them from Geneva, while the Congress was in session. Mrs. Butler's analysis of the difficulties to be encountered in the prosecution of the work of the Federation in the different countries, and of the personnel of the workers, was characteristic, and such as she alone can give. She is not unmindful of America, and views with apprehension, as do we, the tolerated vice of our large cities, with the ominous tendency towards corrupt municipal taxation, as in Omaha and Minneapolis. This hour at the Close, of which we may not properly speak in detail, we shall cherish gratefully as a memorable feature of our brief visit in England."

Valued friendships there were, too, on the Continent, with Mme. Klerck and Count and Countess Hogendorp of the Hague, and other friends in Switzerland.

Bits of travel were among the compensations of these missions abroad. An extract from his editorial correspondence of 1896 gives a glimpse of his great enjoyment of that last journeying in Switzerland:

" BERNE, Switzerland, September 19, 1896.

"Once more we are in Switzerland. This is our fourth visit to this rarely beautiful mountain country. The first was as a tourist, after attendance, as an American delegate, at the first

International Prison Congress, held in London in 1872; the second, as a representative of the New York Committee for the Prevention of State Regulation of Vice, at the first International Congress for the Abolition of State Regulation of Vice, at which the International Federation was organized, held in Geneva in 1877; and the third, at a second Congress, held under the auspices of the Federation, in Geneva, at the close of its first decade, in 1887. * * *

"We left Paris early on the morning of the 7th, for the day trip through Northern France, via Belfort, arriving at Basle, in Switzerland, early in the evening, and spending the night at the Hotel Trois Rois (the Three Kings), on the banks of the Rhine. After visiting a few points of interest in Basle on the morning of the 8th, we journeyed to Lucerne, via Olten, a very old and picturesque Swiss city. Our first view of the snow capped mountains from Lucerne was most refreshing, with a vivid memory of the prolonged, intense and perilous heat through which we had so recently passed in New York! To improve the prevailing pleasant weather for a mountain ascent we left Lucerne on the morning of the 9th for a day and a night on the Rigi, and were greatly favored to have the most enjoyable atmospheric conditions, a not entirely clear sunset view, but a sunrise rare and glorious quite beyond description! Returning from the high mountain, about six thousand feet above the sea level, with its magnificent views of the neighboring still higher Alpine peaks, and of the valleys and lakes below, we made a delightful steamer excursion over the Lake of the Four Cantons to Fluelen and back again to Lucerne. From Lucerne we journeyed by rail over the Brunig pass, and by steamer over Lake Brienz to Interlaken. Modern railroad engineering, wonderfully exemplified by the Rigi, the Brunig, and the Bernese Oberland Railways, over the Wengernalp, has made possible latterly the enjoyment of this grandest of mountain scenery by multitudes with a minimum of fatigue, exposure and cost as compared with former times. The excursion which we made from Interlaken on the 12th inst., a day of a thousand for it, via Lauterbrunnen over the Wengernalp to Scheidegg, the summit, above the snow line of the Jungfrau, the Eiger, the Mönch, and the Wetterhorn, to Grindelwald and return, was, indeed, one long to be remembered! While we were enjoying greatly the refreshing, invigorating upper air at Scheidegg, thousands of feet above Interlaken, we had the pleasant surprise of meeting Prof. James Stuart, M. P., Honorary Secretary of our International Federation, who was also en route with Mrs. Stuart to attend the Berne Conference. After two days of quiet and most grateful rest at Interlaken, the heart of this wonderful mountain region, an added journey of two hours and a half, also a most interesting and pleasant one by rail, part of the way along the beautiful Lake of Thun, brought us safely to Berne, for the International Conference which, representing the American Purity Alliance, we came to attend."

Once more, and for the last time, he crossed the Atlantic, to attend the Congress of 1898 in London, an occasion of very great importance, in the effort to check the reactionary tendency toward restoring the Regulation System in India. *The Shield* (London) in its report of the proceedings of the Congress, says :

"Aaron M. Powell rejoiced that in America as in England the advocates of State regulation of ʋice were becoming more conscious of the inherent sinfulness of the system.   *   *   *

"He most earnestly begged the English people not to set America and the world the bad example of re-enacting a system of State recognition and regulation of vice which on all grounds had been tested, discredited and rejected.   *   *   *

"It was said that the position of women in a country was the measure of the civilization of that country; and he would like to say how his heart had been gladdened in this Congress as in no previous ones to the same degree, by the presence and co-operation of women from the Continent who had added so much to the proceedings. He recalled the first great Congress held in Geneva in 1877, when Eliza Wigham, Mrs. Butler, and Julia Ward Howe spoke for the first time that women's voices had been heard in that city; and it might

now seem like a dream as they gazed on the
enormous progress made since that time. The
voice of Countess Von Hogendorp recalled also
very many and pleasant recollections of the work
of women at the Congress at the Hague; and Mrs.
Butler was, happily, among them still, though not
able to do much in public speaking. It was a
mark of progress that this movement which involved so much for humanity should be so markedly
carried on by men and women working together
as God's children, blessed by His helpful influence
and guidance."

Beside this address as delegate representing the American Purity Alliance, he shared
in the public meeting of the National Vigilance Association of which the Duke of
Westminster is president; and again spoke
briefly in the great public meeting of the
Ladies' National Association held in historic
Exeter Hall, presided over by Mrs. Butler
assisted by Prof. Stuart, M. P. It was a
memorable scene when, at the close of the
meeting, a vote of thanks for Mrs. Butler
having been moved, the vast audience rose;
and amid profound silence, that no syllable be
lost, of the revered but now enfeebled voice,

Mrs. Butler renewed her pledge of faithfulness in these words:

"I cannot make a speech now in Exeter Hall; I am too old. I will only say one thing: in the name and in the strength of our God I promise and vow to the people of England to be faithful unto death in this mission to which God has called me, for the preservation of their dearest liberties and of their holiest aspirations. I thank you, dear friends."

The labors of this Congress were followed by several weeks of restful enjoyment of the beauties of England, shared by his wife and sister. It was plain to see that there must be care not to overtask his physical strength; but this was not allowed to shadow the quiet joys of this season of recreation. On leaving London for the North, a pause was made in the beautiful university town of Oxford. The delightful pilgrimage to the lake country was broken by visits to the hospitable homes of Mr. and Mrs. Wilson of Sheffield, and the Grahams of Dalton Hall at Manchester. The month amid the Lakes in "Wordsworthshire" had, among its satisfactions, cordial intercourse with Canon and Mrs. Rawnsley of Keswick; a "red-letter" day with the "George School Party" under conduct of Jesse H. Holmes; several days with Charles Thompson in his rural home at Morland; and "afternoon tea" with Mr. and Mrs. William H. Hills and their daughter in their lovely "Nook" on Windermere. The last night in the Lake District was spent upon its very edge, in Swarthmoor Hall, so vitally associated with Margaret Fell and George Fox. Then the return journey to London was made memorable, not only by glimpses of old Chester and the mountains and gorges of Wales, but by heart warming welcome to the home of William Edward and Anne Turner in Colwyn Bay; and again, to the sweet hospitality of Mary Radley of Warwick.

The benefit, healthwise, of this summer in England, away from the perilous heat of a city office, and at leisure among scenes of indescribable beauty, was seen during the winter that followed. But to the keen sight of love it was apparent that there was a gradual decline of strength.

The demands of the Social Purity cause constantly increased, and my brother's work in this field was done, for the most part, in addition to his regular engagements. The issue of *Bulletins* began in April 1879 and was continued until January 1886, when the first number of *The Philanthropist* was sent out as a monthly. The arrangements for the World's Purity Congress held in Chicago in 1893 involved very extensive correspondence, and the charge of numberless details.

In 1895 the name of the New York Committee for the Prevention of the State Regulation of Vice was changed to the American Purity Alliance, and the scope of work and membership somewhat extended. A National Purity Congress, continuing three days, was held in Baltimore during October of that year. The representative character and high moral tone of this Congress, fully justified the heavy responsibility and great labor involved in bringing it to a successful issue. So great was the interest awakened by this Congress, it was decided to hold three supplementary Conferences; the first in Philadelphia in November; the second in Boston in December; and the third in New York in January of 1896. Aided by the kindest co-operation of interested workers in each of these cities, the success of the Conferences was most gratifying to my brother. These were followed by the publication, at the cost of great labor, of "The National Purity Congress : Its Papers, Addresses and Portraits "—a volume which might be characterized as a library upon this subject. Those who knew him well will read his life motive and inspiration in the Dedication of this volume :

" To our beloved daughter, in the life beyond, the memory of whose lovely childhood has been a continual inspiration during years of effort to secure improved social conditions and more adequate protection for exposed young girls, the daughters of others, and to promote an equal standard of morality for both men and women, this volume is affectionately dedicated."

For nearly a quarter of a century my brother has used voice and pen in behalf of this cause which touches the very fountains of individual character and of national life. In a few closing words at the Boston Conference, he said:

"Let us keep constantly a high ideal. We believe in God, and we know that with God all things are possible; and in the spiritual resources of the universe there is an answer for every need."

It was in this faith that he labored. It is to the sons and daughters of his soul, up and down the land, that we must look for pens and voices to carry on his unfinished work!

When the word reached his long time friend and co-worker Henry J. Wilson, of his sudden passing to the "larger life" as his own favorite phrase was, Mr. Wilson wrote from Sheffield:

"What can I say! Oh I am so sorry for you, for our cause, for myself! It is twenty-three years since Mr. Gledstone and I were in the States, advised, guided, helped and encouraged by your husband, and ever since he has been doing the same thing for me,—advising, guiding, helping and encouraging,—a most delightful man to co-operate with, a tower of strength to our cause, as to all causes.

And now he is gone, and I feel a tremendous blank!"

If we look for a key to this life of cheerful, unwearying labor, perhaps it may be found in his own closing words at the Boston Conference. He believed in God, and he had found out the life-sustaining secret that "in the spiritual resources of the universe there is an answer for every need." The faith of his fathers, in the indwelling God, the direct personal relation possible to every soul with the All-Father, was his not only as a birthright but through obedience and faithfulness had become a vital faith. Every morning there was a fresh, albeit a silent acknowledgment of this relation to the Divine. Thus was he fortified for what the day might bring of hard work or of perplexing difficulties. And never letting go his hold upon Infinite Love and Infinite Strength, grace was given him to shine away many dark places, and to pass serenely through the difficult ones. Believing that the Everlasting Arms were underneath him, he did not require to see every step of the path before him, but calmly went his way with no dread of the momentary darkness that may be the passage-way to unending day.

> " Life, Death and Immortality
> . Were in his thought of God!"

ELIZABETH POWELL BOND.

TO ONE ARISEN.

In Memory of Aaron M. Powell.

O Friend beloved!   So loving, brave and true!
   So loyal ever to the Spirit's light!
   Who followed duty through the darkest night,
And what thou dared to dream of, dared to do!
How blest wast thou through all thy journey here;
   How blest in that swift, voiceless call, that came
   Like God's own Angel, to bid thee in His name
To come to higher service, His holy presence near.
We loved thy gracious spirit, and now we know,
   Since thou hast been translated, that thou hast
     gone
   Away from us but for a little space:
And He who led thee here and blessed thee so
   We trust will lead us to that Heavenly dawn
Where we shall hear thy voice and meet thee face
     to face.

ISAAC ROBERTS.

AARON M. POWELL AS A RELIGIOUS TEACHER.

WHATEVER other appellation be given to Aaron M. Powell, none could more fully and accurately define his character than that of a Religious Teacher. He was a faithful and consistent member of the Religious Society of Friends, to which his family have belonged as far back as his ancestry has been traced. His membership was with the Stanford Quarterly Meeting, N. Y., until his removal to Plainfield, New Jersey. He grew up in a silent meeting, except for the occasional visits of his uncle, Aaron C. Macy, of Hudson, and other ministering Friends. He was quite young when his interest was aroused in the great work of the liberation of the slaves of our country, by the earnest labors of William Lloyd Garrison, Wendell Phillips, Parker Pillsbury, Charles C. Burleigh, Lucretia Mott,

Stephen and Abby Foster, and the other early Abolitionists. Before he was of age he publicly joined their ranks, and in the anti-slavery work, in which those of various religious denominations were unitedly engaged he was prepared for a broader and more comprehensive labor than that of a religious teacher whose efforts were to be confined within the narrower limits of any one religious organization. It is this fact which makes it proper to refer to it in this consideration of his life as a Religious Teacher. As time passed, and to his anti-slavery labors was added an active interest in the various causes of reform,—Temperance, Peace, Equal Rights for Women, and Social Purity,—he has been constantly ripening, sweetening and broadening for the important Religious service of his later years. He has well learned and zealously and impressively taught the great truth that moral reforms are religious in their character, that morality and religion cannot be divorced without serious injury to both; that, in short, in the simple and expressive language of Matthew Arnold, "Religion is morality touched with emotion." He would thus irrevocably bind together the first and second commandments of our Divine Master, the Love of God, and the Love of our fellow men, and make them both living commandments for practical observance every day. This important truth, of which the world stands so much in need, by his clear and earnest public utterances, and his gentle and winning manner, he has seemed to be one especially commissioned to teach, not alone to any one religious organization, neither his own nor any other, but to the world at large. And he thus furnishes one more distinguished example of the truth of Lowell's words, now more and more generally accepted, but seemingly more prophetic than descriptive of general belief at the time they were uttered:

> "God sends his teachers unto every age,
>   To every clime and every race of men,
>   With revelations fitted for their need."

Thus has he been providentially prepared,

through a long course of thought and training, to become a truly religious teacher, in
the best and fullest modern sense, to the
world in general, regardless of all narrow
sectarian distinctions, and in an especial manner to the Religious Society of his birth and
choice. But he never waited to espouse a
cause until it became popular; and there
were long years during which the views which
he promulgated on reformatory subjects were
not acceptable to all; and even after he was
received as a valuable and impressive teacher
of truths important to the world by those
outside of his own religious society, he was
not yet made wholly welcome by many having influence and authority within its limits.
Thus was he, for a time, a modern example
of the words of our Divine Master:—" A
prophet is not without honor save in his own
country, and among his own kin." But his
time was coming, and how we all rejoice to-
day that he lived to see the change.

A growing uneasiness in the Society,
especially among the younger members, with

the conservative position maintained upon questions of practical interest to humanity, led to outside organizations among them of different kinds, which at length began to find general and somewhat national expression in conferences of members of the various Yearly Meetings, a movement originating largely with Jonathan W. Plummer, of Illinois. These conferences at first included the First day schools, and a little later, the Philanthropic Associations; and at length, in 1894, at Chappaqua, New York, a third was added, called distinctively a Religious Conference. This conference, as already intimated in the reference to Matthew Arnold, was intended to emphasize more fully the union of the emotional with the moral, thus transforming what might be cold and calculating morality into religion. Of this, our first general Religious Conference, Aaron M. Powell was, by universal approval, made the chairman; and no one present during the sessions of that remarkable conference at Chappaqua failed, I am sure, to be most deeply impressed by the profoundly religious character of its sessions, and its solemn close under the wise, well directed and gentle management of its spiritually minded chairman. I am quite sure that many Friends count that meeting in '94 as a period of a new religious awakening to them individually, and it has been such throughout the limits of the Society. What is here said of the Chappaqua Conference, may be said with equal truth of the two conferences since held, that at Swarthmore in '96, and at Richmond, Indiana, in '98. Both of these Religious Conferences were held under the wise and able direction of the same chairman who had, at Chappaqua, proven himself the man divinely appointed for the important place.

Thus has the great importance of his work for the Society, though tardily acknowledged through mistaken conservative influences in the earlier years, been fully and publicly acknowledged in the end, and the whole Society, like a truly bereaved family, is in mourning from one end of the country to the other, and even beyond the sea, for his untimely loss, at a period when, seemingly, his labors were more needed and more important than ever before. But who will presume to decide that question? May not all feel, and in an especial manner the young, who have been so deeply impressed by his pure spiritual influence, that his sudden loss, at such a time, in the very midst of his labors, may really be, in its influence upon the survivors, the crowning sheaf of his glorious labors for society, making them even better known, and adding to their great influence for good? Vainly do we ask, who shall be his successor? Great leaders in the world are unipersonal, they have no successors; although others arise to do, or partially do their work, but in a different way.

> " Gone before us, oh our brother,
>   To the spirit land,
>   Vainly look we for another,
>   In thy place to stand."

EDWARD H. MAGILL.

Swarthmore College, Pa.

IN MEMORY OF AARON MACY POWELL.

Obiit May, 1899.

Men have a life to live, a death to die
    Daily for life according to God's word!
    And unto some the Angel of the Lord
Comes at his hour, they rise without a sigh,
And pass the gates of this mortality,
    To where for welcoming with sweet accord
    The fair forms stand so long from far adored,
Freedom and Temperance, Peace and Purity.

And thou hast risen and gone the silent way
    Dear friend! whose hand—albeit it left the plow
    For fields of barren discord, bitter scorn—
Sowed seeds of love we gather here and now,
Thou too hast passed the doors of wider day
    But left our greater darkness less forlorn.

H. D. Rawnsley.

Keswick, England.

NOT CREED, BUT CHARACTER. [1]

GROUNDS OF SYMPATHY AND FRATERNITY AMONG RELIGIOUS MEN AND WOMEN.

By AARON M. POWELL.

IT is in behalf of one of the smaller religious bodies, the Society of Friends, that I am invited to speak to you. In the time allotted it would be quite impossible to cover exhaustively the whole field of my broad subject, "The Grounds of Sympathy and Fraternity Among Religious Men."

It is altogether natural and proper that in form and method and ritual there should be diversity, great diversity, among the peoples interested in religion throughout the world; but it is also possible, as it is extremely desirable, that there should be unity, fraternity and co-operation in the promulgation of simple spiritual truth. To illustrate my thought I may say that not very long ago I went to one of the great Salvation Army meetings in New York with two of my personal friends, who were also members of the Society of Friends. It

[1] An address before the Religious Congress for Friends in the World's Parliament of Religions held in Chicago in 1893.

was one of those meetings full of enthusiasm with volleys innumerable, and we met that gifted and eloquent Queen of the Army, Mrs. Ballington Booth, to whom I had the pleasure of introducing my two Quaker friends. Taking in the humor of the situation, she said: "Yes, we have much in common; you add a little quiet and we add a little noise."

The much in common between these two very different peoples, the noisy Salvationists and the quiet Quakers, is in the application of admitted Christian truth to human needs. It is along that line that my thought must lead this morning with regard to unity and fraternity among religious men and religious women. Every people on the face of the earth has some conception of the Supreme and the Infinite. It is common to all classes, all races, all nationalities ; but the Christian ideal, according to my own conception, is the highest and most complete ideal of all. It embraces most fully the Fatherhood of God and the brotherhood of mankind.

Justice and mercy and love it maintains as due from each to all. There are no races, there are no territorial limitations or exceptions. Even the most untutored have always been found to be amenable to the presentation of this fundamental Christian thought exemplified in a really Christian life. Here I may illustrate by the experience of William Penn among the Indians of North America. He came to them as their brother and as their friend, to exemplify the principles of justice and truth. It is a matter of history that the relations between Penn and the Quakers and the Indians have been exceptional and harmonious, on the basis of this ideal brotherhood of man. Alas, that all the Indians in America might not have had representatives of this Quaker humane thought to deal with! What a different page would have been written in American history!

Many years later another Friend was sent out under President Grant's administration to labor as a superintendent among the Indians, the noble hearted, true Quaker, Samuel M. Janney. As he went among the Indians committed to his charge, he not only undertook to deal with them with reference to their material interests, but he also sought to labor among them as their friend, and in a certain sense as a religious helper and teacher. He talked with those Indians in Nebraska about spiritual things. They could understand about the Great Spirit as they listened to him, and he told them furthermore, the wonderful story of Jesus of Nazareth, commending His teaching and the lesson of His life and His death to them. They listened, with regard to the Son, as they had with reverence to the Father, but he could not impress them, in the face of their sad experience with a so called Christian nation, with the virtues of the Son.

Finally one old chief said to him: " We know about the Father, but the Son has not been along this way yet."

I do not wonder, in the light of the record which this so called Christian nation had made in dealing with those Indians, that they thought that they had never seen the Son out that way yet. It is, alas, to our shame, as a people, that it must be said as a matter of historic truth, that the very reverse of the Christian spirit has been the spirit shown in dealing with the Indians, who have been treated with bad faith and untold cruelty.

A fresh and living instance of this spirit is illustrated in the chapter we are now writing so shamefully in our dealings with the Chinese. We are sending missionaries abroad to China, but what are we teaching by example in America with reference to the Chinese except the Godless doctrine that they have no rights which we are bound to respect ? We are receiving lessons, valuable and varied, from these distinguished representatives of other religions, but what are we to say in their presence of our shortcomings, measured by the standard of our high Christian ideal, which recognizes the brotherhood of all mankind and God as the common Father ?

I want to say that the potential religious life—and it is a lesson which is being emphasized day by day by this wonderful parliament—is not a creed, but character. It is for this message that the waiting multitude listens. We have many evidences of this. Among the recent deaths on this side of the Atlantic which awaken world-wide echoes of lamentation and regret, there has been no one so missed and so mourned as a religious teacher in this century as Phillips Brooks.

One thing above all else which characterized the

ministry of Phillips Brooks was his interpretation of spiritual power in the life of the individual human soul. The one poet who has voiced this thought most widely in our own and in other countries, whose words are to be found in the afterpart of the general program of this parliament, is the Quaker poet, Whittier. His words are adapted to world wide use by all who enter into the spirit of Christianity in its utmost simplicity. In seeking the grounds of fraternity and co-operation, we must not look in the region of forms and ceremonies and rituals, wherein we may all very properly differ, and agree to differ, as we are doing here, but we must seek them especially in the direction of unity and action for the removal of the world's great evils.

I believe we stand to-day at the dividing of the ways, and whether or not there shall follow this parliament of religions any permanent committee, or any general organization, looking to the creation of a universal church, I do hope that one outcome of this great commingling will be some sort of action between the peoples of the different religions, looking to the removal of the great evils which stand in the pathway of the progress of all true religion.

Part of my speech has been made this morning by the eloquent ex-governor who preceded me, but I will emphasize his remarks with regard to arbitration. There were two illustrations of my thought to which he did not make specific reference. One is recent in the Behring Sea arbitration.

What a blessing that is as compared with the old fashioned method of settling the differences between this country and Great Britain by going to war. We may rejoice and take courage in this fresh illustration of the practicability of arbitration between two great and powerful nations.

I may cite also one other illustration, the Geneva award, which at the time it occurred was perhaps even more remarkable than the more recent arbitration of the Behring Sea dispute. Among the exhibits down yonder at the White city, which you doubtless have seen, is the great Krupp gun. It is a marvellous piece of inventive ingenuity. It is absolutely appalling in its possibilities for the destruction of humanity. Now, if the religious people of the world, whatever their name or form, will unite in a general league against war and resolve to arbitrate all difficulties, I believe that that great Krupp gun will, if not preserved for some museum, be literally melted and recast into plowshares and pruning hooks.

This parliament has laid very broad foundations. It is presenting an object lesson of immense value. In June I had the privilege of assisting here in another world's congress, wherein were representatives of various nationalities and countries. We had on the platform the distinguished archbishop of St. Paul, that great liberal Catholic, Archbishop Ireland. Sitting near him was Father Cleary, his neighbor and friend—another noble man. Sitting near those two Catholics was Adjutant Vickery, of the Salvation Army, the representative of Mrs.

Ballington Booth, who was unable through sickness to be present. Near these there were several members of the Society of Friends, and along with them were some Episcopalians, Methodists, Baptists, Presbyterians and one Unitarian whose face I see here to-day. All these were tremendously in earnest to strike a blow at one of the great obstacles to the progress of Christian life in Europe—state regulated vice.

I cannot deal in detail with that subject now, but I may say that it is the most infamous system of slavery of womanhood and girlhood the world has ever seen. It exists in most European countries and it has its champions in America, who have been seeking, by their propagandism, to fasten it upon our large cities. It is one of the most vital questions of this era, and it should be the care and responsibility of religious people everywhere to see that as speedily as possible this great shame shall be wiped away from modern civilization.

Let me tell you an incident that occurred in Geneva, Switzerland, three or four years ago. There jumped out of a four-story window down to the court below a beautiful young girl. Marvelously her life was spared. A noble Christian woman, whom I count it a privilege to number among my personal friends, went to this poor girl's side and got her story. In substance it was this:

She had been sold for a price in Berlin to one of the brothel keepers of Geneva, and, as his property, had been imprisoned in that brothel, and was held therein as a prisoner and slave. She endured it as long as she could, and finally, as she told this friend of mine, "When I thought of God I could endure it no longer and I resolved to take the chances of my life for escape," and she made that fearful leap, and providentially her life was spared. What must be the nature of the oppression that will thus drive its victims to the desperate straits of this young girl? It is a slavery worse than the chattelism, in some of its details, which formerly prevailed in our own country.

Now, what has America to do on this line? America has a fearful responsibility. Though it may not have the actual system of state regulation, we call ourselves a Christian country, and yet, in this beloved America of ours, in more than one state, under the operation of the laws called "age of consent," a young girl of ten years is held capable of consenting to her own ruin. Shame, indeed; it is a shame; a tenfold shame. I appeal, in passing, for league and unity among religious people for the overthrow of this system in European countries, and the rescue and redemption of our own land from this gigantic evil which threatens us here.

I now pass to another overshadowing evil, the ever pressing drink evil. There was another congress held here in June; it was to deal with the vice of intemperance. I had the privilege of looking over forty consular reports prepared at the request of the late Secretary of State, Mr. Blaine. In every one of these reports intemperance was shown to be a producing cause of a large part of the vice, immorality and crime in those countries. There is need of an alliance on the part of religious people for the removal of this great evil which stands in the pathway of practical Christian progress.

Now, another thought in a different direction. What the world greatly needs to-day in all countries is greater simplicity in connection with the religious life and propagandism. The Society of Friends, in whose behalf I appear before you, may fairly claim to have been teachers by example in that direction. We want to banish the spirit of worldliness from every land, which has taken possession of many churches, and inaugurate an era of greater simplicity.

The actual progress of Christianity in accordance with its ideal may be stated, in a sentence, to be measured by the position of women in all lands. The Society of Friends furnished pioneers in the prisons of Old England and of New England in the direction of Divinely inspired womanhood. We believe there is still urgent need of an enlargement of this sphere to woman, and we ought to have it preached more widely everywhere. There should be leagues and alliances to help bring about this needed change. The individual stands alone, unaided, comparatively powerless; but in organization there is great power, and in the fullness of the life of the spirit, applied through organization, it is possible to transform the world for its benefit in many directions.

Some one has described heaven as being simply a harmonious relationship between God and man.

If that be a true description of the heavenly condition, we need not wait until we pass beyond the
river to experience something of the uplift of the
joy of salvation. Let us band together, religious
men and women of all names and nationalities, to
bring about this greater harmony between one
another and with God, the Father of us all.
Then, finally, in all lands and in every soul, to the
lowliest as well as the highest, may this more and
more become the joyous refrain of each, "Nearer,
my God, to Thee; Nearer to Thee."

9 783744 714693